THE REFINING ROOM

DEVOTIONAL MEMOIR: 90-DAY JOURNEY FOR WOMEN BREAKING, BECOMING & BEING SET-APART

Josette Fleury (Blossom Refined)

DEDICATION

To the One who refined me, restored me, and called me His own.

Jesus Christ, my Savior, my Healer, and my Refiner.

Every page in this book is a tribute to Your faithfulness.

To my daughters, Nia, Sarayah, and Delicia, and my precious granddaughter, Kylie.

You are my heart, my legacy, and my joy.

May you always walk in purity, purpose, and the confidence of being chosen by God.

To every woman who has ever been broken in silence, refined in hidden places, or called to rise when she felt unprepared.

This book is for you.

May you discover the beauty of surrender and the strength of being set apart.

May your refinement lead you into glory.

ACKNOWLEDGMENTS

First and foremost, I give all glory, honor, and praise to my Lord and Savior Jesus Christ, the Refiner of my soul and the Author of my story. He entrusted me with this assignment, and every word in these pages was birthed in His presence. This book is my offering back to Him.

To my incredible editor, Jan, thank you for standing with me through every draft and late-night revision. Your patience, skill, and heart have shaped this work with excellence.

To my beautiful daughters, Nia, Sarayah, and Delicia, and my sweet grandgirl, Kylie, you are the light that motivates me to keep pressing forward. You remind me daily that legacy begins at home. Mommy loves you deeply and eternally.

To my man of God, Prophet Isaac Lanquaye, thank you for believing in me, for your love, your counsel, your covering, and your unwavering faith. Your prayers and prophetic encouragement strengthened me in seasons when my spirit felt weary. I honor the God in you.

To my beloved friend, Nuefy, thank you for being my safe place. You have seen me vulnerable, stretched, and refined, yet you loved me through each stage with grace and loyalty.

To my little sisters in Christ, Evelyn, Versatile, Duchess, Gwen, and Shiku-wa, your prayers and sisterhood have been a consistent blessing. Our connection is proof that Kingdom family transcends time and distance.

To my brothers in Christ, Emeka, TikTok Pastor, TikTok Psalmist, and Pastor Prince, thank you for your intercession, encouragement, and covering. Your obedience to God has blessed many, including me.

To my dear friends, Nessa, Marie, Cindy, Ludie, Daphney, Aisha, Delle, Deandra, Dr. Anne, Kinji, and Dr. Sherley, thank you for loving me, praying for me, and walking beside me through refining seasons. You celebrated every testimony that rose from the fire.

To my SPU doctoral cohort sisters, Ashley, Juanita, and Deanna, your brilliance and faith inspired me to keep pressing toward purpose, even when my load felt heavy.

To my sweet cousin and goddaughter, Nerlande, and to my admiring aunt, Solange, thank you for believing in my calling and encouraging me when I questioned my strength.

To my amazing parents, Mr. and Mrs. Joseph Fleury, thank you for the example of Christian living, for your prayers, and for teaching me to surrender my life to Jesus Christ. The values you planted in me continue to bear fruit.

To every soul who prayed, sowed, spoke life, or believed in this mission, thank you. Your love became oil that fueled my obedience.

To God be all the glory.

FOREWORD

A new wind of the Holy Spirit is moving through this generation. It is subtle yet strong, quiet yet undeniable, and it is calling women into deeper identity, purity, and purpose. This book arrives in that very moment, offering guidance for women who have endured trials, carried silent battles, and longed for a place where their pain and purpose could finally speak the same language.

Life unfolds in seasons that test, stretch, and transform us. Some seasons arrive with gentle lessons. Others come with breaking points that touch the deepest parts of who we are. Hardship, loss, disappointment, and emotional overwhelm are not signs of abandonment; they are invitations to grow. In every period of shaking, something sacred is being formed. Growth takes root in places where comfort once lived, and strength rises in moments when the heart feels fragile.

Across this era, women are awakening to the truth of who they were designed to be. They are learning resilience through adversity and discovering wisdom through surrender. Challenges such as illness, grief, or failure often press them into deeper reliance on God. These refining moments strengthen faith and awaken a confidence that does not come from circumstances but from divine identity. This book honors that process. It reminds every woman that she carries a calling, a distinct voice, and a divine uniqueness that cannot be replaced.

Through personal testimony, spiritual insight, and heartfelt reflection, this work guides women into a clearer understanding of themselves and their purpose. It teaches that refinement is not meant to break you. It is designed to build you. It pushes you out of survival and into becoming. Robert Tew once wrote, "The struggle you are in today is developing the strength you need for tomorrow." Those words speak to the heartbeat of this book: every struggle holds the seed of strength, and every refining process carries the promise of transformation.

Before you move deeper into these pages, I invite you to honor the author, Josette Fleury Of Blossom Refined. Her writing carries compassion, courage, and conviction. She speaks with the authority of someone who has walked through the fire and returned with oil for others. She does not simply recount experiences; she offers revelation. Her voice reminds women that their battles have meaning, their growth has purpose, and their calling is worth protecting. She shines a light on the truth that nothing in your life is wasted when placed in the hands of God.

As you read this book, may you feel seen, strengthened, and stirred. May you find courage to embrace every chapter of your life, from the breaking to the becoming, and finally to being set apart. Allow these pages to remind you that God has been writing your story with intention. Each trial sharpened you. Each breakthrough shaped you. Each moment prepared you for the woman you were created to be.

Step forward with confidence. Your refining has purpose. Your growth has value. Your calling waits for your yes.

May this book lead you into that yes with faith, wisdom, and holy expectation.

—**Prophet Isaac Lanquaye**

CONTENTS

INTRODUCTION

There was a version of me that looked whole on the outside while my soul lived quietly in pieces. I carried responsibilities with a steady face, yet something within me kept breaking in places I never spoke about. I pushed through days with strength that felt borrowed and cried through nights that felt endless. Still, God was shaping something beneath every hidden fracture. The refining began long before I recognized it, rising through silence, struggle, and surrender. This book rises from that refining. These pages hold the moments when God reached for me long before I knew how to reach back.

This book will walk you into transformation that begins in unseen places and rises into every part of your life. You will discover how refinement forms identity, how wilderness seasons create clarity, and how breaking becomes the doorway to healing and awakening. This book will guide you through the shift from survival to purpose, from silence to prophetic identity, and from carrying wounds to carrying oil. You will learn how obedience matures, how the hidden place becomes holy ground, and how the voice of God becomes clear when everything else grows quiet. As you read, you will awaken to what God is already stirring within you.

I wrote this book from a place of surrender, not perfection. The Lord tugged on the parts of me I once hid: the wounds, the silence, the unspoken fears, the patterns that did not match the identity He gave me. Through tears and repentance, He revealed that my testimony carried an assignment. The ache that pushed me to write came from watching women survive storms without language for what they survived. God insisted that the refining He did within me was not for me alone. It was meant to guide daughters who are ready to rise, ready to heal, and ready to be sealed for glory. This book carries that mandate. It is written from process, from honesty, and from faith that grew in dark rooms where only God saw me.

My life moved through stages that felt impossible to survive. The breaking came first, through childhood wounds, fractured confidence, and seasons that emptied me completely. The crushing followed, through illness that weakened my body, isolation that exposed hidden idols, and the severing of ties that once felt unshakeable. Refinement pressed me until every false identity began to fall away, revealing the woman God was forming underneath the pain. In that quiet, the awakening began. I discovered identity as daughter, learned obedience that stretched deeper than emotion, and recognized the prophetic calling that God had placed on my life long before I understood it. Then came the releasing. A mantle settled, ministry opened, and visibility increased. This shift did not come from striving. It came from surrender. My story moved from survival to assignment. If God restored what was broken in me, He can restore everything concerning you.

Each chapter follows a clear structure to help you apply truth as soon as you receive it. Memoir Moments offer honest scenes from my life that reveal how God refined me through practical, ordinary places. Devotional Insights root the lessons in Scripture, giving you stability and clarity. Interactive Encounters invite you to practice stillness and hear God personally. Prophetic Declarations speak life into your atmosphere. Journal Prompts help you process what the Holy Spirit is revealing. Closing Prayers seal each chapter with intimacy and alignment. This is not simply a book. It is a companion for your refining, guiding you into deeper identity, purity, and purpose.

Now the focus turns to you. You have survived storms only God understands. You have carried battles quietly and rebuilt yourself without applause. Heaven has seen every step you took when no one else noticed. God is already working beneath the surface of your heart. These chapters will help you recognize His voice, His hand, and His invitation. This is not entertainment. This is encounter. Expect God to reveal what needs healing, what needs releasing, and what needs awakening. Expect clarity. Expect peace. Expect transformation. You will not close this book the same way you opened it.

May your spirit awaken to the God who calls you chosen and seen. May your heart soften in the places where survival once hardened you. May every chapter stir fresh oil, fresh faith, and fresh identity. The refining hand of God rests on you with purpose. You are stepping into a season where confusion gives way to clarity and fear gives way to strength. Take a breath. Open your heart. The refining has already begun.

PART ONE: THE BREAKING

WHERE FALSE IDENTITY IS STRIPPED, AND THE WILDERNESS BEGINS.

Chapter 1
THE GIRL WHO SURVIVED

P runing feels cruel when you're in it. Rejection, humiliation, silence each cut stings and leaves you wondering if anything good can grow from the loss. But pruning is not punishment. It is God's way of removing what cannot remain, so that what He planted in you has space to thrive. The Gardener never wastes His shears. Every cut has a purpose.

For me, pruning began before I understood the word. I was a Haitian American girl in Brooklyn, caught between two worlds too Haitian for classmates, too American for family traditions. Teased in school, pressured at home, and silenced by fear, I learned early to perform, to survive, to hide the wounds that shaped me. Yet even then, God was near. His hand was steady on the shears, trimming lies I had mistaken for truth.

This chapter is about those first cuttings. It is about the girl who felt invisible and the God who reminded her she was never unseen. If you've ever questioned whether rejection meant abandonment, I invite you into these pages. What felt like breaking was the beginning of becoming.

Where is God asking you to embrace your identity in Him above all else?

Memoir Moments

Brooklyn had its own rhythm; horns blaring on Utica Avenue, the thud of basketballs echoing from cracked pavement, corner bodegas spilling out the smell of fresh bread and baked patties. Languages collided on every block: Creole in one ear, Spanish in the other, English pressed in between. The borough was alive, fierce, and unapologetic; for a Haitian American child, it was also a place that could wound.

Inside our two-bedroom apartment in Crown Heights Brooklyn, life carried the warmth and weight of tradition. My mother's Creole prayers rose from the kitchen as pots of diri ak pwa simmered, mingling with the sweet aroma of fabulosa from her constant cleaning. My father's voice carried authority; his rules set the boundaries of our world. Church was not optional; it was the center of life. Sundays stretched from morning service to youth ministry in the evening, while the rest of the week moved to the rhythm of Wednesday Bible Study, Friday night prayer service, and Saturday youth choir rehearsal. In our home, school, church, and family were the pillars that held everything together.

But outside those walls, I was marked as different. In classrooms and on playgrounds, "Haitian" was hurled like an insult. Names like "boat people" and cruel rumors about AIDS clung to us like shadows. The teasing cut deep, and I learned early how to shrink; how to keep my head down so the ridicule would pass faster.

Being the first American-born child carried its own weight. I became my mother's interpreter before I could write in cursive explaining symptoms to doctors, translating bills at the bank, reading labels at the grocery store. Sometimes I felt proud, like I was doing something important. Other times the stares reminded me how foreign we appeared; how fragile belonging really was. Responsibility taught me maturity but it also whispered that my worth was tied to what I carried.

Two worlds pulled at me daily: the proud, prayer-soaked Haitian household that demanded resilience and the harsh American streets that mocked what made us different. Between them, I learned silence and I learned survival. And though I could not see it then, every cut was shaping me. It was here God began pruning me, even when I didn't have words for it.

In our household, life was measured by three pillars: school, church, and home. My parents believed that if we excelled in those spaces, everything else would follow. They had left Haiti with little more than faith and determination and they expected their children to climb higher than they ever could. Education was not optional. Faith was not casual. Home was not flexible.

My father carried a strict sense of order that often felt unyielding. Pants, nail polish, and lipstick were forbidden for my sisters and me. Male friends were discouraged because he believed they brought distraction. His rules were meant to protect but at times they pressed me into silence. I learned that obedience equaled honor and honor equaled love.

At school, the weight of performance became my armor. Each A on a report card felt like a shield against shame. Every achievement told me I was safe for another season. I believed that as long as I stayed ahead, no one could call me less than. What I did not realize was how quickly performance can become a prison, locking you into a cycle where worth is always earned but never secure.

The Church, too, carried pressure. My father made sure we had a deep reverence for the Lord and learned to honor Him in our daily lives. He wanted us to take God seriously, reading our Bibles, praying faithfully, and living with integrity. For me, it sometimes felt like suffocating under a system of rules without knowing the God behind them. I sang in the choir and attended every prayer service, but my understanding of grace was shallow. I thought God loved me because I was useful, because I behaved, because I looked the part. I did not yet know He loved me simply because I was His.

Caught between Haitian customs and American culture, between religion and relationship, between pride and shame, I learned to perform in every space but rarely to rest in who I was. I wondered, who was I really outside of what I achieved?

Siblings and Silent Rivalries

Growing up, our home carried unspoken expectations, quiet comparisons, and invisible hierarchies only siblings understand. I was the second daughter, the first born in America, and for most of my early life, I believed I was the first child until I learned about Esther.

Esther, my older sister, was born and raised in Haiti. I met her when I was nine and she was twelve. For so long, I thought I was the center of my parents' dreams and ambitions, but Esther had lived a whole story before mine began. When she migrated to America at eighteen, we became two sisters learning how to love one another while wrestling with identity, distance, and silent resentment. Our relationship was strained at first. I did not know where to place her in my heart, and she did not know how to embrace the little sister who unknowingly took her place in our parents' story.

Then came James my brother, my almost twin. We were only eleven months apart, sharing birthdays close enough to blend and childhood adventures laced with rivalry. Everyone said we looked alike, talked alike, and thought alike. But behind those similarities lived tension. I was often celebrated for my academic success while he carried the sting of comparison. Over time, jealousy quietly took root. He grew closer to our younger sister, and I became the dependable achiever, the example. My wins sometimes felt like losses to him.

Ruth was the youngest, nine years behind me, a free spirit with a world all her own. I loved her deeply, though our age gap made our closeness feel more protective than peer-like. When Esther joined us in America, Ruth bonded with her and James, while I remained the steady one, watchful, responsible, and holding things together.

Through it all, I learned that family is not always defined by closeness it is shaped by survival. I survived comparison, invisibility, and the ache of being loved for what I did more than for who I was. Yet even in those fractures, God was shaping me for compassion, grace, and the healing that comes when forgiveness takes root.

Survival in my own house trained a calm smile that looked like strength. I carried that same stillness back into the hallways of school and the rows of church.

The hallways of school were battlefields I never asked to enter. The insults came sharp and unrelenting *"Haitian booty scratcher,"* "boat person," "HIV carrier." They rolled off tongues like casual jokes, but each word landed heavy. My cheeks burned, my throat tightened, and I learned to hold my tray steady in the cafeteria while staring at the table instead of the faces around me. Silence became my shield. If I stayed quiet, if I kept to the corners, maybe I could avoid the next round of laughter at my expense.

When I was five, another wound carved itself into my sense of worth. The teachers at my Catholic school decided I was not ready for first grade. I was told to repeat kindergarten. No one explained the reasoning in a way my young mind could understand. What I did understand was shame. It felt like being marked "not enough" before I had even started. From that point, achievement became my shield. Every grade, every award, every perfect report card was proof I belonged, even if deep down I feared it could all be stripped away again.

Home carried its own discipline. My father believed in order and did not hesitate to enforce it with the belt. I told myself it was love, because that was what I had been taught, but the painful marks left behind told another story. After a visit from a social worker, the physical punishment stopped, but the silence it planted inside me remained. I learned to shrink myself, to make as little noise as possible, to stay in line.

Over time I became skilled at disappearing. If emotions rose, I buried them. I wore the mask of the "good one," the achiever, the fixer. It looked like strength, but it was survival.

Even in the midst of ridicule, there were moments when I felt set apart in ways I could not explain. Sometimes classmates would curse or use profanity, then turn to me with an apology. They sensed something different, even when I could not name it. I had not yet fully given my life to Christ, but His presence was already resting on me.

Even in silence, God saw me. Even in rejection, He was near.

One of my earliest memories of God's nearness came during a night of fear. A fire broke out in our building and the hallway filled with smoke and darkness. My mother clutched my younger brother, wrapped in a sheet, while calling out in Creole, "Josette, kote-ou ye la? which means where are you?" I answered back, "Mwen la," which meant "I am here." Step by step, I held the handrail and walked blindly down the stairs, trusting that each movement would carry me closer to safety. I could not see the way out, but something within me believed we would make it through. Without fully understanding, I was learning what it meant to lean on God.

Years later, at fifteen, I entered the baptismal waters of my church. My heart pounded as I prepared to go under. I had grown up in a Christian household, but this felt different. I could not yet grasp the fullness of salvation, but when the water covered me, I felt a weight lift from my shoulders. It was as though God Himself was answering a question I had not known how to ask. That moment became an anchor I would return to again and again.

Music deepened that sense of His presence. In the choir, surrounded by voices, I found a freedom I rarely felt at school. One Sunday we sang a simple hymn, nothing grand, just a steady melody that rose like a prayer. I closed my eyes and felt the notes wrap around me. For the first time, I did not need to perform to be loved. I only needed to be present.

At school, I felt invisible. At church, I felt seen.

I didn't know it then, but those whispers were the beginning of His pruning love.

Devotional Insight

God's Purpose in Family Tension: John 15:1–2

"I am the true vine, and My Father is the gardener. He cuts off every branch in Me that bears no fruit, while every branch that does bear fruit, He prunes so it will be even more fruitful."

Pruning is not punishment; it is preparation. The shears cut close, but they cut with intention. Every removal is purposeful. Every restriction is strategic. Every uncomfortable season is evidence that the Father is shaping something deeper than comfort. He is shaping character.

When I look back on my childhood, I now recognize the Gardener's hand in places I once resented. The bullying at school, the shame of repeating kindergarten, the cultural pressure, and the silence in my home all felt unbearable. I assumed those moments meant I was unworthy. I believed rejection proved God had overlooked me. But those were the very places His pruning began.

He used each cut to remove lies I had carried for years:

- the lie that my worth depended on performance

- the lie that my culture made me less

- the lie that silence was safer than honesty

What looked like loss was actually God clearing away what could not remain in my future. He was not breaking me. He was preparing me.

Childhood and Calling: Psalm 139:13–16

"All the days ordained for me were written in Your book before one of them came to be."

Your childhood does not disqualify you; it equips you. The moments you would erase often become the soil where identity is planted. God uses family tension, misunderstanding, and even cultural pressure as tools to refine purpose.

Where I saw failure, God saw formation. Where I felt overlooked, God was cultivating resilience. What felt like abandonment became the place where He strengthened my dependency on Him.

Identity Through Pruning: Romans 8:14–16

"The Spirit Himself testifies with our spirit that we are God's children."

Performance never proves identity. Jesus did not redeem you to make you a performer; He made you, His daughter. Pruning is the Father's way of stripping away every false identity so you can rest in the truth of who you already are.

Where shame once rooted itself, He planted dignity. Where fear controlled me, He planted courage. Where silence suppressed my voice, He planted boldness.

Family tension became a classroom. Every strained bond became a lesson in unconditional love. Every conflict became training in patience, empathy, and spiritual maturity.

Purpose in Pain: Genesis 50:20

"You intended to harm me, but God intended it for good."

When you are set apart from those closest to you, God is often teaching you to stand secure in Him. Isolation inside a family often feels like rejection, but it can be divine refinement.

Survival in those seasons is not only emotional; it is spiritual. It is choosing forgiveness over resentment. It is choosing presence over withdrawal. It is choosing to be shaped instead of hardened.

You survived because God had more for you to become.

For You

Pruning is not evidence of God's absence; it is proof of His love.

What He trims, He intends to strengthen.

What He removes, He replaces with life.

What He asks you to release was never meant to define you.

If He is cutting something away, it is only because He sees fruit you cannot yet see.

Pruning is proof that you are loved enough to be shaped.

The Refining Room (Interactive Encounter)

Prophetic Declarations

Speak these aloud over your life. Let your own voice become the sound of agreement with Heaven.

- I declare I am never abandoned; God is always near.

- I declare my heritage is a gift and a calling.

- I declare the chains of unworthiness are broken.

- I declare every wound is healed in Jesus' name.

- I declare my voice brings life to those who feel invisible.

- I declare survival turns into thriving.

- I declare nothing from my past can cancel my destiny in Christ.

- I declare pruning prepares me for greater fruitfulness.

Journal Prompts

Take time to write with honesty and openness. These prompts are meant to help you reflect on pruning moments in your own life and to see them through the eyes of grace.

1. Think of a childhood moment when you felt unseen. Where can you now recognize God's presence in that memory?

2. If you could speak the truth to your younger self, what would you say? Write it as if you are writing her a letter.

3. Have you ever felt compared to a sibling, friend, or peer? How did that affect your sense of identity?

You have seen behind the surface now. Her distance had reasons. Her silence had history. Her hesitation had roots. She was never rejecting you. She was protecting herself. Avoidant attachment does not come from coldness. It comes from a lifetime of learning that closeness felt unsafe.

A man who understands this pattern already separates himself from the rest. You are not guessing in the dark anymore. You are watching her behavior through the lens of psychology and the wisdom of lived experience. This is how strength becomes strategy. This is how clarity replaces confusion.

Before you move forward, carry one truth with you: her reactions were formed long before you arrived. Your role is not to repair her past. Your role is to understand the terrain you are walking into. And now that you see the pattern, it is time to see its roots.

The next chapter gives you the blueprint behind her guarded heart. Once you understand the origin, you will understand the woman. Turn the page. Her childhood answers the questions her adulthood keeps asking.

Closing Prayer

Father, thank You for the pruning seasons in my life, even the ones I resisted and did not understand. Thank You for removing the lies that once held me captive and for planting truth where shame once lived. I praise You for being near in every chapter of my story, even when I could not recognize Your hand. Teach me to remain rooted in You when pruning comes again. Give me the courage to release false identities and to let go of everything You never intended to define me. Show me how to rest in Your presence when the cutting feels sharp. Remind me that Your hand is both steady and gentle, that what You remove You always replace with something alive. May my story give courage to those still in their own pruning season, and may they see that You are near to the brokenhearted. **Amen.**

Chapter 2
WHEN GOD LET ME WANDER

The wilderness is no punishment; it is the silence where idols lose their grip. Outwardly, I kept moving, teaching classes, paying bills, and holding smiles in place. Inside, the well ran dry. I chased love that looked safe, mistook attention for care, and pressed on without counsel, convinced that effort could heal emptiness. The more I performed, the quieter my spirit felt, as if God had stepped back and let my choices speak. Yet mercy kept circling me, even when I ignored the warnings and rushed ahead. The ache of loneliness, the sting of regret, the hum of busyness that never satisfied all of it exposed what I trusted more than Him. This season felt like exile, but it became an encounter. In the quiet, God began stripping pride, bitterness, and the need to be seen, so I could finally hear Him again. This is where wandering revealed what worship truly means.

This is the story of when God let me wander, so I could finally find Him.

Memoir Moments

Chasing Love and Spiritual Emptiness

There was a time when I chased love with everything I had, believing it would fill the empty spaces inside me. I told myself that as long as the person said they believed in God and went to church sometimes, it was enough. I never stopped to ask if they truly loved Him, or they never asked if I did... I thought attendance at church equaled alignment with God.

I was young, restless, and afraid of being alone. Every relationship felt like proof that I mattered. I mistook attention for care and commitment for love. I prayed for connection but ignored conviction. The idea of waiting for God's timing seemed too slow, so I created my own. Each time, I ended up more drained than before. Sleep slipped away, joy faded, and my spirit felt dry. I would wake up next to someone and still feel alone.

Looking back, I realized that I was searching for something holy in places that could never hold it. My faith had form but not fire. I went through motions, sang the songs, lifted my hands, yet my heart stayed guarded. I was chasing affection when I needed transformation. The longing I tried to quiet with people was actually a hunger for God.

That hunger was not for a man. It was for meaning.

Lack of Guidance and Counsel

I still remember the voice of my youth leader before I walked down the aisle for the first time. She looked at me with gentle concern and said, "If he's not the right one, you can still wait." Those words should have stayed with me, but impatience had already taken root. I believed marriage would fix the emptiness I carried. Waiting felt like wasting time, and I wanted proof that I was chosen, loved, and secure.

Her warning was not controlling; it was compassionate. She saw what I could not. I mistook her wisdom for interference and brushed it aside. My heart was already made up, and my pride drowned out discernment. I told myself that love was enough, that as long as he believed in God, everything else would fall into place. But faith without maturity cannot sustain a covenant.

Years later, I would recall her words and feel their truth settle deep within me. Waiting would have spared me from a storm I was not equipped to weather. Back then, I called it love, but now I see it was longing, an attempt to fill a spiritual void with human affirmation. The pain that followed was not God's cruelty but the consequence of my own unwillingness to listen.

To every woman who rushed into something without guidance, you are not alone. Many of us ran ahead of God's timing, confusing approval with love and attention with commitment. Wisdom often comes before experience, but we usually recognize it only after the damage is done.

But God's mercy often waits on the other side of our unheeded wisdom.

Mistakes in Marriage and Motherhood

The test came sooner than I expected. I was still in podiatric medical school when I discovered I was pregnant with my firstborn. The two faint pink lines on the test blurred as I held it in my shaking hands. The acceptance letter for podiatric medicine still hung on the wall of my first apartment, proof of a dream I thought was solid. That night I sat on the edge of my bed, thinking about my parents, my church, and my future. Fear filled the room, heavy and still. The girl who had once felt so confident suddenly felt very small.

I left school before the semester ended and returned to New York City. What looked like failure then was a redirection that only makes sense now. Motherhood came quickly and fiercely. My focus shifted from textbooks to baby bottles. My days became filled with early mornings and long nights, teaching during the day and caring for my child after work. My daughter Nia became my reason to keep moving. Even when I felt forgotten, God was present, quiet but constant, providing what I could not yet pray for.

Years later, my first marriage brought hope that faded too fast. The man I trusted betrayed me. His deceit cut deep, emotionally, financially, and spiritually. Divorce court felt like a graveyard for the dreams I had carried. I packed boxes in silence and wondered if restoration was still possible for someone like me. Yet, even then, God's mercy waited behind the loss.

When my daughter grew up, she repeated a pattern I had prayed would end. She had a child at almost the same age I had her. Watching that unfold broke something inside me, yet it also opened my eyes. Cycles reveal where grace must begin. I stopped blaming myself and started asking God to rewrite what shame had written across generations.

My mistakes in marriage and motherhood were real, but so was God's faithfulness. He never left. His mercy reached into every wrong decision, every painful ending, and turned them into lessons of grace. What I once called failure became the soil where compassion began to grow.

Tenderness is what remains when the storm passes. Compassion is what grows when you finally forgive yourself.

Impact of Early Career and Faith

Teaching became both my refuge and my burden. The classroom smelled of chalk dust and pencil shavings, the air humming with restless energy as teenagers filled their seats. Mornings began before sunrise. I packed lunches, reviewed lesson plans, and prayed for enough strength to make it through the day. My voice carried over the chatter of students reciting multiplication tables, while fatigue pulsed behind my smile.

Each afternoon ended with stacks of graded papers and the faint hum of fluorescent lights overhead. The walk to my car often felt heavier than the books I carried. I loved my students and believed in what I taught, but beneath the dedication was a quiet exhaustion that never fully lifted.

Spiritually, I was split in two. There were moments when worship songs stirred something alive in me, when Scripture felt clear and close. Then there were weeks when my Bible stayed shut on the nightstand, when prayers were whispers fading into sleep. I told myself I was too busy, but in truth, I was spiritually dry. I had traded communion for competence, presence for productivity.

There were nights when I sat at my kitchen table after grading papers, my daughter asleep in the next room, wondering when my faith had become another task to manage. I had learned how to care for others while quietly neglecting my own soul.

The classroom taught me patience and purpose, but it also revealed how easy it is to pour out until you are empty. I realized that faith cannot survive on obligation alone. It must be nourished, not performed.

I was teaching others but forgetting to be taught by God.

Mistaking Survival for Love

The move to Georgia was supposed to be a fresh start. The air felt different there, heavy with humidity and promise. I rented a small apartment that smelled faintly of old carpet and fresh paint. The walls were thin, the ceiling fan wobbled when it turned, and the paycheck from my new job barely covered the bills. I told myself I was starting over, but what I was really doing was surviving.

It was during that season that I met him. He helped me unpack boxes, fixed things around the apartment, and filled the silence I had been running from. I mistook his attention for stability. Loneliness will often dress itself as love when your spirit is tired enough to believe it. At first, he made me feel chosen. Soon, his charm became control, and my dependence deepened into fear.

On social media, we looked perfect. Smiling photos, dinner dates, captions full of faith and affection. Behind closed doors, the silence between us grew louder. I was present in his world, yet unseen in his heart. He paraded me publicly but dismissed me privately. Every apology came with conditions, every promise with manipulation. Still, I convinced myself this was love. I called it love, but it was only survival with a soundtrack.

That relationship exposed a deeper truth. I was not just fighting for him; I was fighting to prove I was worthy of being kept. I believed that endurance equaled loyalty, that staying made me strong. But God had other plans.

When the relationship ended, the loss felt like collapse, yet it was mercy disguised as heartbreak. God began dismantling the counterfeit, stripping away every false version of love I had accepted. What I thought was rejection was actually rescue.

Sometimes God allows something to fall apart so you can finally see what was never whole.

Lessons from the Wilderness

The wilderness stripped away everything I thought made me strong. Pride fell first, quietly, without warning. Then came the bitterness I carried from betrayal and disappointment. God began peeling back layers I had built for protection, exposing motives I did not want to see. What I once called confidence was really control. What I called independence was often fear disguised as strength.

Loneliness became my teacher. I learned that silence could heal what words cannot. There were nights when I felt unseen, and mornings when I woke up wondering if my prayers still reached heaven. Yet even in the emptiness, there was something sacred forming. God was refining what pain had distorted.

He took away the pettiness that came from old wounds and the unforgiveness that hardened my heart. He replaced it with compassion, patience, and the ability to see people through His eyes instead of through my pain. The wilderness is not a punishment; it is a process. It is where God removes what you thought you needed so He can give you what will last.

Every season of isolation revealed a lesson. I learned that peace is not found in people or success, but in surrender. The tears, the silence, the waiting, none of it was wasted. God was not breaking me; He was building me again.

I entered empty and came out refined.

The Three Seasons of Motherhood

Pruning prepared me for motherhood long before I knew I would carry that title. The same hands that held me through rejection would one day hold me through labor pains, divorce papers, and whispered prayers over sleeping children. I didn't plan for any of it, yet God wrote every chapter with purpose I could only see in hindsight.

Nia: The Fearful Girl Learning to Survive

The test came sooner than I expected. I was twenty-three when I discovered I was pregnant. The two faint pink lines on the test blurred as I held it in my shaking hands. My acceptance letter to podiatric medical school still hung on the dorm wall, a dream I thought was certain. That night, I sat on the edge of my bed thinking about my parents, my church, and my future. Fear filled the room. The confident girl who once believed she had control suddenly felt very small.

I withdrew from podiatry medical school before the semester ended and returned to New York. What looked like failure then was actually redirection. Motherhood came quickly and fiercely. My focus shifted from textbooks to baby bottles, from study groups to midnight feedings. My firstborn, Nia, arrived in 2001, and with her came both a storm and a sunrise.

Her father and I were never married, though we shared a home for a time. When I realized our hearts were not aligned, I packed my belongings and moved to Atlanta, determined to build a better life. Single motherhood was not glamorous. It was a series of quiet sacrifices, long commutes, and whispered prayers. But in that season of lack, God met me. He provided in ways I didn't even know to ask for.

Nia faced her own challenges in school, learning struggles that tested our patience, but she persevered. Her quiet strength mirrored mine. When her father passed away at sixteen, she was just beginning to rebuild their relationship. Watching her grieve the loss of what might have been broken me, yet even there, God was teaching me that closure does not always come through conversation but through surrender.

Sarayah: The Hopeful Woman Believing Again

Ten years later, I believed love had returned to stay. At thirty-three, I married with hope in my heart and faith in forever. Two years later, I gave birth to my second daughter, Sarayah, the only one of my girls born inside of wedlock. She entered the world with fire in her eyes and excellence in her spirit. Self-driven and discerning, Sarayah rarely needed to be pushed, only guided.

Her father lived nearby, but life dealt him a hard blow when diabetes led to a leg amputation. Watching Sarayah navigate his illness while still excelling in school reminded me that resilience is often inherited, not taught. She carried determination in her DNA.

That marriage, filled with promise, ended two years later. Betrayal came quietly but left me in pieces. I packed boxes again, now with two hearts to protect, hers and mine. Yet even in heartbreak, God's mercy did not leave me. Every closed door became a reminder that protection sometimes looks like loss.

Delicia: The Wiser Mother Learning Peace

Five years passed before love found me again. At thirty-eight, I gave birth to my last daughter, Delicia, in 2016. Her arrival felt like a divine surprise, a final chapter I never expected to write. After her birth, I tied and burned my tubes, believing motherhood had reached its completion. But even that decision carried God's signature of sovereignty.

Delicia was born into both joy and exhaustion. Her father and I were married, but he lived abroad in Trinidad and Tobago. Our love stretched across borders and time zones. Her birth was a paradox, filled with both laughter and longing. I wanted stability; God wanted surrender.

Delicia became my mirror of grace. She was free-spirited, brilliant, and quietly confident. Teachers often said, "She knows more than she shows." When she scored a four in ELA and a three in Math on her state exams, I smiled through tears. Her intelligence wasn't loud, it was layered. She reminded me that not every gift announces itself loudly. Some brilliance blooms in stillness.

Three Daughters, Three Decades, Three Versions of Me

Nia at twenty-three, the fearful girl learning to survive.

Sarayah at thirty-three, the hopeful woman believing in love again.

Delicia at thirty-eight, the wiser mother learning peace after pain.

Each of them reflects a different chapter of my evolution. Motherhood did not just change my life; it refined my soul. It taught me that strength is not measured by how much you endure, but by how gently you love while enduring.

When Nia became a mother around the same age I had her, I felt the ache of repetition. It was as if history circled back, asking whether I truly believed God could break generational patterns. Watching her carry the same weight I once bore was painful. Yet that is where grace met me again.

God whispered, "Stop blaming yourself. This is where redemption begins."

I realized then that every mother carries both legacy and lesson. We cannot choose how our children's stories unfold, but we can choose how we respond to ours. I stopped calling my motherhood messy and started calling it holy. Every sleepless night, every broken marriage, every tear shed over my daughters' futures became soil for something sacred to grow.

My mistakes in marriage and motherhood were real, but so was God's faithfulness. He never left. His mercy reached into every wrong decision, every painful ending, and turned them into lessons of grace.

What I once called failure became the foundation of compassion.

What I once called shame became a testimony of survival.

What I once called broken became beautiful.

Tenderness is what remains when the storm passes.

Compassion is what grows when you finally forgive yourself.

Devotional Insight

The Wilderness and the Word: Deuteronomy 8:2

"Remember how the Lord your God led you all the way in the wilderness these forty years, to humble and test you in order to know what was in your heart."

The wilderness is not a punishment but a proving ground. God uses it to humble, not humiliate. He allows lack so that dependence becomes real. He allows silence so that obedience grows deeper than emotion. The wilderness exposes what words often hide.

I once thought those barren seasons meant I had fallen out of His favor. When dreams collapsed and prayers seemed unanswered, I assumed I had failed Him. But the truth is, the wilderness is where He leads those He loves. It is where God removes every illusion that something else can satisfy. He does not send us there to destroy us but to strip us of pride, false identity, and misplaced trust.

Formation Through Fire: 1 Peter 1:6–7

"These trials will show that your faith is genuine. It is being tested as fire tests and purifies gold."

When I found myself a single mother after walking away from medical school, I saw failure instead of formation. I thought the detour disqualified me from purpose. Later, when divorce broke my heart, I mistook the pain for divine rejection. When I juggled teaching, motherhood, and exhaustion, I thought God had forgotten my dreams. What I could not see then was that each of those moments was a refining fire. The pruning that began in my childhood continued through motherhood.

Grace in Motherhood: Isaiah 40:11

"He tends His flock like a shepherd; He gathers the lambs in His arms and carries them close to His heart."

Motherhood became its own wilderness, an altar that revealed both my limits and His limitless grace. Every child entered my life with divine purpose: one taught me patience, another taught me faith, and another reminded me that joy is still possible after heartbreak. God used each of them to show me that love is both weight and worship. My story as a mother was never about perfection; it was about perseverance. God never demanded flawlessness; He invited partnership. When I handed Him my fears, He handed me His peace. When I released my regrets, He released my redemption.

Rebuilding the Heart: Psalm 34:18

"The Lord is close to the brokenhearted and saves those who are crushed in spirit."

The wilderness humbles by revealing how fragile our self-made foundations are. When relationships failed, I saw how much of my worth depended on being chosen. When career doors closed, I realized how much I trusted achievement to prove my value. God let those things fall apart, not because He was angry, but because He was merciful enough to rebuild me correctly.

Every detour, whether through loss, parenting struggles, or broken plans, has a divine purpose. Every disappointment hides an invitation to deeper faith. You may not have been the perfect mother, but you have always been chosen. Chosen women carry both pain and promise. God uses detours to destroy shame, mercy to mend what pride broke, and grace to lead us home.

For You

If you are standing in a dry place wondering what went wrong, remember, God is not punishing you; He is preparing you. He has not forgotten you; He is forming you. The wilderness is where He removes what you thought you needed so He can give you Himself. And that will always be enough.

The Refining Room (Interactive Encounter)

Prophetic Declarations

- I decree that every generational cycle in my family line is broken and redeemed by the power of grace.

- My daughters will not repeat my pain, they will reap my prayers.

- I am not defined by my mistakes but refined by God's mercy.

- Restoration flows through my bloodline; what began in fear will end in favor.

- I walk in the confidence that God is parenting me as I parent others.

Journal Prompts

1. How has motherhood, or nurturing others, revealed areas where God wanted to heal you?

2. Which generational patterns have you seen in your family, and how is God breaking them through you?

3. What do you want the legacy of your motherhood or mentorship to sound like when your story is told?

Take a few moments to write your answers with honesty. Each question is an open door to freedom. The wilderness will not last forever, but the wisdom it gives will remain for a lifetime.

The wilderness was never meant to destroy me; it was meant to refine me. Every silence, every stripped place, every unanswered prayer became the soil where trust was planted. What once felt like isolation became invitation, and what looked like loss revealed God's lasting mercy. I entered weary but left renewed, learning that His presence is the greatest provision of all.

The next season would test that renewal through love that looked holy but was not. Yet even there, grace waited. The wilderness didn't end me. It introduced me to the God who rebuilds from ruins.

Closing Prayer

Father, thank You for never leaving me, even when I wandered far from Your will. You saw the pride, the fear, and the need to control, yet You chose mercy over judgment. Forgive me for chasing approval, for mistaking survival for love, and for settling where You called me to grow. Thank You for the wilderness that stripped away everything false so I could see You clearly. Teach me to rest in Your timing and to trust Your pruning hand. Let every broken season become proof of Your restoration power. I surrender my past, my plans, and my pain to You. Lead me forward in truth, rooted in grace. In Jesus' name, **Amen.**

Chapter 3
WHEN LOVE WASN'T HOLY

Some loves feel like redemption at first but end up revealing what you refused to heal. I once believed that love would fix what faith had not yet touched. Every promise sounded like prophecy; every apology felt like proof that things were finally changing. I prayed over what God had already warned me to release. I called desire "purpose" and attachment "commitment." I was searching for holy love in unholy places.

Memoir Moments

I wanted a love that felt like safety, yet I accepted one that demanded silence. I mistook emotional comfort for divine confirmation. I stayed because leaving felt like failure, not realizing that disobedience wears the same disguise as devotion when you are afraid to be alone. My heart wanted holiness, but my habits kept pulling me toward what was familiar.

God had been whispering through every red flag I ignored. Each argument, lie, and empty apology was a sermon I refused to hear. When everything finally collapsed, I saw what He had been showing me all along. Love without holiness is not love at all. It is idolatry dressed as intimacy, and it always costs more than it gives.

This is the story of when God let me see the difference.

Prophetic Red Flags

I saw the warnings early, but I mistook them for challenges that love could conquer. There were nights when silence filled the room louder than any argument, and I convinced myself that tension meant passion. I prayed for peace but kept choosing chaos. Every time God whispered "leave," I found a reason to stay. I thought patience was proof of faith when it was really fear of being alone.

The first marriage began with distance, both physical and spiritual. We were separated by miles, yet I believed commitment could close the gap. Phone calls started with affection and ended with accusations. When his tone turned sharp, I called it stress. When my spirit felt uneasy, I called it normal. There were nights when I cried after we hung up, asking God for clarity but my heart was too attached to obey what He was already saying.

The second marriage carried the same pattern, only dressed in different words. We argued until the sound of my own voice felt foreign. He called me names, and I returned them with silence. I was losing myself under the weight of keeping something God had not built. The Holy Spirit had been waving red flags while I was painting them white. I convinced myself that prayer after disobedience would make disobedience holy.

Emotional immaturity ruled both of us. I expected a man to heal what I refused to surrender. There were days when I searched his phone, hoping to find the truth but always uncovering heartbreak. Every unanswered call became evidence that my spirit already knew the truth. Yet I stayed.

I told myself that God would honor my effort, but He was asking for my obedience, not my endurance.

Respect had left the relationship long before I admitted it. We cursed, we competed, and we called it communication. Every argument chipped away at the version of myself that once believed love meant prayer, patience, and partnership. We never prayed together, never opened Scripture together, and never asked God to lead us. I prayed privately for a public miracle. But no miracle grows in soil where pride is planted.

Years later, I saw how disobedience carries its own echo. The voice of God had not been silent; I simply stopped listening. He spoke through exhaustion, through tears, through friends who told me the truth. He even spoke through the uneasiness I felt when my peace went missing. Every ignored warning became a seed of consequence.

Looking back, I understand that my desire to be loved blinded me to what love required. Real love does not destroy peace. Real love does not demand compromise with sin. God was not trying to punish me by removing what I wanted. He was trying to protect me from becoming what I feared.

When everything finally fell apart, I saw that I had never lost love. I had lost alignment. And alignment with God is the only soil where love can grow.

The Weight of Soul Ties

A soul tie is an invisible chain, soft enough to feel like closeness, strong enough to hold you hostage. I didn't understand what it was while I was living in it. I only knew that every time I tried to move forward, something pulled me back. Even when I knew the relationship was toxic, my emotions refused to let go. I mistook obsession for love and pain for passion. The more I tried to convince myself that I was happy, the more my peace withered.

Each tie began the same way, with comfort. Conversations that made me feel seen, hands that promised safety, words that sounded like prayer but carried no anointing. It felt like a connection, but it was contamination. I thought intimacy meant agreement, yet what I agreed to were spiritual contracts written in sin. Every physical act outside of the covenant became another strand woven into the chain around my spirit. I wasn't just connected to a person; I was entangled with their pain, their habits, and their demons.

The illusion of love held me longer than the reality of truth. I told myself that I could fix it, that my loyalty would heal what was broken. I prayed for God to bless what He never ordained. I was emotionally exhausted and spiritually numb. Days blurred together as I went through motions that looked like commitment but felt like captivity. I would wake up thinking about him, scroll through messages that I knew were lies, and still answer when the phone rang. That was not love. That was bondage disguised as belonging.

I thought I was choosing companionship, but I was feeding an addiction. Each apology, each temporary reconciliation, became another dose that kept me hooked. I called it love because admitting it was sin would have meant facing my part in the pain. I lowered my standards in the name of grace, not realizing that grace never requires compromise. My worth began to shrink under the weight of what I was settling for. The woman who once knew her value was now questioning if she deserved anything better.

Guilt followed every moment of weakness. I would pray after sin, promising God that it would not happen again, yet the pattern continued.

The soul tie made me think repentance was a reset button instead of a realignment. I wanted forgiveness without separation, healing without obedience. I cried on Sunday mornings and sinned on Sunday nights. My heart was divided, and a divided heart cannot hear the voice of God clearly.

Every time I ignored conviction, the tie tightened. My emotions became louder than the Holy Spirit. When I let sin choose my connections, I let the enemy counterfeit my covenant. What looked like love was actually manipulation wrapped in charm. I kept trying to save what God was asking me to surrender. The truth was simple but painful: I had been loyal to dysfunction because it felt familiar.

There were nights I would lie awake replaying every conversation, trying to make sense of it all. The silence after an argument felt unbearable. I'd reach for my phone, knowing that reconciliation would cost me more of myself. I began losing focus, losing joy, losing parts of my identity. My mind was filled with confusion, my prayers were shallow, and my spirit felt heavy.

I was surviving on emotional crumbs, convinced that the little I had was better than being alone.

When I finally allowed God to speak into the chaos, He revealed that love tied to sin can never produce freedom. He showed me how every act of compromise opened the door for deception. I had let my heart make decisions that my spirit had to pay for. God could not heal what I kept holding onto.

Breaking those ties required surrender that felt like death. I had to stop replaying memories, delete numbers, and release fantasies of what could have been. I had to allow God to fill the emptiness that I had once filled with false intimacy. That process felt lonely, but it was the beginning of liberation.

God began to show me that He could not heal what I refused to release. Once I opened my hands, He began to open my heart. What had once chained me became the testimony of His power to free. The invisible chains fell one by one, until all that remained was peace.

God's Call to Surrender

I was in my room when conviction hit like a holy earthquake. It came without warning, yet everything in me knew it was time. The air felt heavy, as if heaven itself was waiting for my answer. I had run from the truth long enough. Every distraction, every relationship, every compromise had lost its power. I sat on the edge of my bed, heart pounding, tears sliding down my face, realizing that God was calling me to surrender completely. This was not about a man or a mistake. It was about my soul.

I had built my life around survival, not submission. My strength had become my shield, my pride, my comfort. When the Holy Spirit whispered, *"Enough,"* I felt stripped bare. Conviction burned deeper than shame. I thought surrender would mean losing control, but it was the moment I began to regain it. The presence of God filled that room, not to condemn me, but to cleanse me.

Fasting became my first weapon. I turned down plates and turned up prayer. Every craving reminded me of how much I had depended on the wrong things for satisfaction. The first few days were hard. My body wanted food, but my spirit wanted freedom. With each fast, I felt God peeling away layers I had used to protect my pain. He confronted the idols I had built relationships that replaced His presence, habits that dulled conviction, and pride that kept me pretending I was fine.

Prayer became my second weapon. At first, it was awkward. My words stumbled, and my mind wandered. But soon, prayer became air, I could not breathe without it. Some nights I prayed in silence, other nights I cried until I fell asleep. I began to understand that surrender was not about losing, it was about being found. God was reclaiming the territory my disobedience had surrendered to the enemy.

He asked me to let go of fornication, alcohol, and anything that numbed the ache in my spirit. I poured out bottles, deleted contacts, and closed every open door to sin. It felt radical, but obedience always looks extreme to those still in compromise. The nights felt quiet, but they were sacred. Every sacrifice became an altar.

Forgiveness was harder. I thought I had moved on, but bitterness hid behind my prayers. God revealed how resentment was still shaping my reactions. I had to forgive those who betrayed me and forgive myself for allowing it. Deliverance came one confession at a time. I renounced the soul ties that had kept me bound and called back every piece of myself I had given away. The warfare was intense. Memories surfaced, dreams replayed, and emotions fought to regain control. But the blood of Jesus silenced every accusation.

There were moments I questioned if holiness was possible after such a past. But God reminded me that grace is not fragile, it is fierce. His mercy was not a second chance; it was a complete reset. Surrender did not strip me, it sanctified me. The woman who once bowed to desire now bows only to the voice of God. What once controlled me no longer had access to me. My appetites changed, my focus sharpened, and my heart finally rested.

I made a covenant with God that night. I promised purity not as a performance but as worship. I put on my ring of celibacy and asked Him to guard my heart until He decided it was time to love again. It was not about punishment; it was protection. I learned that obedience births peace faster than compromise ever could.

Fasting and prayer no longer felt like rituals, they became weapons and refuge. My tears turned into testimony. The same hands that once held pain were now lifted in praise. I was no longer trying to earn God's approval. I was living in it.

That night, I finally cut the soul ties. The silence that followed sounded like peace. It was the sound of chains falling, the sound of heaven celebrating one daughter who finally came home.

Devotional Insight

Love Out of Order: 1 Corinthians 13:4–6

"Love does not delight in evil but rejoices with the truth."

I learned the hard way that love outside of God's order can never reflect God's heart. I chased relationships that looked good but lacked godliness. I prayed over connections God never ordained and tried to bless what He never built. Every compromise left my spirit emptier than before. When love is not rooted in holiness, it becomes idolatry wrapped in emotion. God used every red flag to draw me back to Himself, showing me that real love whispers truth, not confusion.

The Cleansing of Conviction: Psalm 51:10

"Create in me a clean heart, O God, and renew a right spirit within me."

These words became my lifeline. I wanted love so deeply that I accepted counterfeits. I mistook compromise for connection and emotion for discernment. But conviction was mercy, not condemnation. God was not exposing me to shame me, He was inviting me into purification. Repentance became a cleansing process, washing away what my spirit could no longer carry. I learned that a clean heart cannot thrive in old habits. Surrender became the doorway to restoration.

Honoring the Temple: 1 Corinthians 6:19–20

"Your body is a temple of the Holy Spirit... you are not your own; you were bought at a price."

For years, I treated my body as if it belonged to love rather than the Lord. I used intimacy to prove worth, not realizing I was giving away sacred ground. When I understood that my body carried the presence of God, everything shifted. Purity was no longer about perfection; it was about purpose. It became an act of reverence, a declaration that I belonged to God before I belonged to anyone. With each obedient choice, peace followed.

Breaking the Unequal Yoke: 2 Corinthians 6:14–18

"What fellowship can light have with darkness?"

Soul ties taught me how deeply relationships shape the spirit. Every connection carries a consequence, toward God or away from Him. I yoked myself to people who were not aligned with my calling, and their battles became mine. Breaking soul ties felt like breaking chains, not because I was rejecting them, but because God was redirecting me. Separation was not abandonment. It was deliverance. God cannot fill what is still full of yesterday's residue.

Surrender Before Freedom: James 4:7

"Submit yourselves to God. Resist the devil, and he will flee from you."

Submission was my greatest struggle because I wanted control. I wanted love on my own terms. But freedom required surrender. Once I submitted, strongholds that felt unbreakable began to fall. Temptations that once felt irresistible lost their grip. The closer I moved to God, the clearer I heard His voice. He was not withholding love. He was protecting my purpose.

For You

Maybe you have stayed in something God never signed His name to. Maybe you have mistaken comfort for covenant. You are not alone. Conviction is not God pushing you away; it is God pulling you back. Let Him clean what you tried to hide. Let Him heal what others broke. The love that comes after surrender will not drain you, it will define you. You are chosen, seen, and deeply loved.

The Refining Room (Interactive Encounter)

Prophetic Declarations

- I will sever every counterfeit covenant and refuse to settle for anything that keeps me bound.

- My past partnerships cannot poison my purpose because God has already redeemed my story.

- I choose purity over pain and truth over temporary satisfaction.

- I am worthy of holy love, the kind that honors God and protects my peace.

- God is rewriting my story in righteousness, and I will walk in alignment with His will.

- Every soul tie that once held me captive is broken by the blood of Jesus.

- I release every emotional chain that has limited my growth.

- I declare that my heart is free, my body is sacred, and my future is secure in God's hands.

Journal Prompts

1. What prophetic red flags did you once ignore, and what made it difficult to let go at the time?

2. Which emotional or spiritual ties still need cutting, and what step can you take today to release them?

3. How can purity become your protection rather than a restriction in your walk with God?

Take time to sit with these questions and write your honest answers. Let the Holy Spirit guide your thoughts as you reflect. Healing begins when truth is no longer avoided. God is not asking for perfection; He is asking for surrender. Every time you release something that once defined you,

He replaces it with purpose. The same power that broke my soul ties is available to you right now. Trust that what He removes, He intends to redeem.

The same God who exposed my idols restored my intimacy with Him. What once felt like loss became the doorway to freedom. Every broken attachment, every moment of shame, and every tear I cried was used by God to rebuild me into a woman who walks in truth. I learned that love without holiness cannot last, but love rooted in Him will never fade.

When I finally released the counterfeit, Heaven called me home. God replaced my confusion with clarity and my compromise with conviction. The wilderness of unholy love was never meant to destroy me; it was preparing me for revelation. What once wounded me became the soil where purpose began to grow.

This is where surrender turned into identity. This is where I stopped chasing love and started becoming His daughter.

Closing Prayer

Lord, I surrender the parts of me that once settled for less than Your best. I bring every soul tie, every memory, and every relationship that kept me bound, and I lay them at Your feet. Cleanse my heart from the residue of sin and shame. Teach me how-to walk-in purity, not out of fear, but out of reverence for Your presence.

Cut every connection that was not ordained by You. Heal the parts of me that were shaped by broken love. Restore my mind where confusion lived and fill every empty space with Your peace. I repent for every time I chose comfort over conviction. Give me strength to walk in obedience, even when it costs me what I once desired. Thank You for covering me with grace and calling me worthy of holy love. In Jesus' name, **Amen.**

Chapter 4
HEAVEN CALLED ME DAUGHTER

Heaven did not call me "Daughter" when I was strongest. It called me when I finally stopped running. The moment came quietly, not in a church service or during a conference, but in the stillness of my room. My back was against the wall, and every place I had tried to hide had failed me. Tears flowed until words could not form. What I later came to understand as liquid prayers began to pour from my soul.

Memoir Moments

I had spent years performing for love, trying to prove that I was faithful, disciplined, and worthy. I prayed with passion but carried guilt in silence. I called it faith, but it was striving. I thought God wanted perfection, but He wanted presence. In that quiet moment, I heard Him whisper through my tears, "Enough. Stop running. You are still Mine." Those words wrapped around my heart and broke every lie I had believed about my worth.

That night was not a ceremony; it was an encounter. Shame lifted, guilt dissolved, and peace took its place. I was not earning love anymore. I was resting in it. This chapter is about that moment, when Heaven spoke identity over my brokenness and called me what I had always been: His daughter.

First Prophetic Word

The first time I felt Heaven speak identity over me, I was not in a crowd waiting for a prophetic moment. It came quietly, in a season when I was still untangling from sin and shame. I had been carrying guilt, trying to prove to God that I could do better, but deep down I felt unworthy to even speak His name. My life was in transition, and I was still learning what surrender really meant.

That day, I was praying my liquid prayers. My words had run out, so I sat in silence. Then came a thought so clear, it silenced the noise in my mind: *You are still Mine.* It was not thunder or lightning, but a soft voice that pierced through the heaviness I wore. The words settled in my spirit like they had always been there, waiting for me to believe them. For the first time, I realized that God had not changed His mind about me.

That was the prophetic word that shifted everything. It did not flatter me; it located me. It found me in the middle of repentance and spoke belonging instead of judgment. I was still learning how to pray through pain, still breaking free from old habits, but His voice named me before my behavior could catch up. In that moment, I understood grace differently. I was not earning a title. I was finally hearing the truth about who I had always been.

Deep Conviction & Internal Shift

Conviction came like a whisper that carried weight. It was not loud, but it was undeniable. I had reached the end of pretending that partial obedience was enough. Every distraction, every secret habit, every excuse was exposed in the quiet of that moment. I heard the words in my spirit, *enough is enough.*

Stop running.

Stop numbing.

Start surrendering.

The Holy Spirit began to show me the areas I had been protecting. Fornication that I called weakness. Grudges that I justified as boundaries. Guilt that I carried like it was humility. I realized that I had been managing sin instead of allowing God to cleanse me. I wanted control over my own healing, but control had become my cage.

This conviction did not crush me. It uncovered me. I felt a holy sorrow rise, not because I was worthless, but because I had been living beneath what grace had made available. Tears came again, but they felt different. They were not born from shame; they were the release of a woman who had been running from her own redemption.

In that stillness, I finally yielded. I let God have the parts of me I had tried to fix on my own. The shift was invisible but absolute. The striving stopped, and surrender began.

Spiritual Dreams Begin

After my encounter with God, dreams began to come more often. They were not confusing or dramatic. They were simple, but they carried meaning. Each one felt like a private conversation between my spirit and Heaven. Sometimes I would wake up with a phrase or image that lingered through the morning, and I knew it was not from me. It was God's way of continuing the conversation He had started in prayer.

One night, I dreamed of being washed in clear water that kept flowing no matter how much I tried to hold it. I woke up with tears in my eyes, knowing the Lord was showing me cleansing. It was not about shame. It was about renewal. I prayed for understanding and opened my Bible to Psalm 51:10: *Create in me a clean heart, O God, and renew a right spirit within me.* That verse confirmed what the dream meant. It was time to let go completely and stop trying to manage what He was ready to heal.

The next day, I obeyed in a small but real way. I removed things that had tied me to old habits and relationships. It was not easy, but it was necessary. Each act of obedience made the air feel lighter. The dreams continued, reminding me that God was speaking even when I was asleep. They became gentle tutoring from a Father who was teaching His daughter how to listen again.

School Building Leader Season

When I became a school leader, the weight of responsibility was heavy. I carried keys that opened every classroom and office, but inside, I still felt locked out of peace. I spent my days organizing meetings, supporting teachers, and managing students, yet I often returned home drained. I had the title of authority, but I struggled to believe I was truly equipped for it. Every compliment from colleagues felt undeserved, and every mistake felt like proof that I did not belong.

I was leading a building while God was rebuilding me. The confidence I showed during the day often crumbled at night. I prayed for wisdom, but underneath the prayers lived a quiet ache, a belief that I had to prove my worth to everyone, including God. The orphan spirit whispered that love had to be earned and that rest was weakness.

As I grew in leadership, the Lord began to confront that lie. Through fasting and repentance, He showed me that authority without identity leads to exhaustion. I learned that I could not lead effectively while doubting my place in His heart. Slowly, daughterhood began to settle in me. I was no longer surviving from approval but serving from acceptance. God was teaching me that being called "daughter" was the highest position I would ever hold.

Deliverance Hunger & Private Encounter

Deliverance came in a quiet room, not in a crowd or under anyone's hand. I had reached the end of pretending to be strong. The tears would not stop, and I did not try to hold them back. My body trembled as the weight of years poured out in silence. Those tears were liquid prayers, groans that spoke louder than any words I could form. Heaven understood them.

It reminded me of a child's cry when a parent knows the reason without being told. In that moment, I sensed the Holy Spirit translating every tear into a plea for help. I felt surrounded by presence, not condemnation. The voice of God was soft but clear: *You are still Mine.* Shame lifted like dust swept away by wind. Guilt that once followed me dissolved, and the orphan spirit that had chained me for years broke. Peace filled the room.

I realized I had been fighting for an identity that had already been given to me. God had not waited for my perfection to claim me. He met me in repentance and wrapped me in belonging. I was not promoted to daughter; I was received. It was not earned; it was embraced. In that sacred stillness, adoption became real. I knew then that I was no longer a servant begging for mercy but a daughter standing in grace.

Devotional Insight

Love without identity will always feel like striving. I learned that truth the moment God whispered, *you are still Mine.* That single word carried the power to rewrite my entire story. Prophecy does not decorate; it defines. It names you before your behavior can qualify you.

Known and Set Apart: Jeremiah 1:5

"Before I formed you in the womb I knew you, before you were born, I set you apart."

Those words reminded me that God's knowledge of me came long before my failures did. My first prophetic word was not a reward for getting it right; it was a reminder that He had chosen me before I knew how to choose Him. Identity precedes performance. The Holy Spirit used that moment to anchor my heart in truth: I was known, loved, and claimed.

From Orphan to Adoption: Romans 8:15; Galatians 4:6

The orphan spirit taught me to survive through striving. I tried to earn love through discipline and self-control. But Romans 8:15 says, *"You received the Spirit of adoption, by whom we cry, Abba, Father."* Adoption does not start with achievement; it begins with surrender. Galatians 4:6 adds, *"Because you are sons, God sent the Spirit of His Son into our hearts, crying, Abba, Father."* The orphan reflex keeps you suspicious of grace. It whispers that you must prove your worth before you are accepted. But the daughter reflex trusts access over approval. It rests in the truth that the Father's love cannot be negotiated.

The Father's Nearness: Psalm 34:18

"The Lord is near to the brokenhearted and saves those who are crushed in spirit."

I saw this scripture come alive in my own deliverance. When I could not form a prayer, my tears became language. The liquid prayers that flowed from my soul were understood by Heaven. God met me, not in my perfection, but in my pain. The nearness of the Father is not measured by distance but by dependence. The moment I stopped hiding my weakness, His presence filled the room.

Hearing Again: John 10:27

"My sheep hear My voice, and I know them, and they follow Me."

When repentance became real, I began hearing God again. His voice came through dreams, through scripture, and through quiet impressions that carried peace. Each word was a call back to alignment. The Lord never stopped speaking; I had just stopped listening. Hearing Him again was the sign that intimacy had been restored. The same Spirit who convicts also comforts. His voice does not accuse; it confirms identity.

Cultural vs. Kingdom Identity

As a Haitian American woman, my culture taught me to fight, to survive, and to prove strength in every situation. Kingdom identity, however, trained me to surrender. Culture told me to keep moving; Kingdom told me to rest in purpose. Culture celebrated independence; the Kingdom called me into dependence on God. My roots tell me who I am; His Kingdom tells me whose I am. I learned that I could honor my culture without letting it define my calling. The Holy Spirit refined what was strong but misaligned and turned it into submission that honors God.

Renewed Mindset: 2 Corinthians 5:17

"Therefore, if anyone is in Christ, the new creation has come: The old has gone, the new is here."

This truth became my lifeline. I realized that deliverance was not only about what I left behind but also about what I was becoming. New creation thinking replaced old guilt patterns. I no longer viewed myself through my past decisions but through His redemption. Every day became a chance to live as someone made new, confident, clean, and covered by grace.

For You

Maybe you have been striving to earn what God already calls yours. Maybe you have believed that your mistakes disqualified you from daughterhood. Let these truths settle in you:

- You are known.

- You are set apart.

- You are not forgotten.

- You are loved without condition.

The Refining Room (Interactive Encounter)

Prophetic Declarations

- I am not what I have done. I am who God says I am.

- I renounce the orphan spirit and receive the Spirit of adoption.

- I trade performance for presence and punishment for peace.

- My cultural strength bows to my Kingdom calling.

- I hear my Shepherd's voice, and confusion breaks now.

- I am kept, covered, and called, beloved and becoming.

- I am chosen, set apart, and loved without condition.

Journal Prompts

1. Where have your tears already said what words could not?

2. What part of your cultural identity do you deeply value, and how will you surrender it to align with Kingdom identity this week? Choose one act that honors both heritage and holiness.

3. What simple act of obedience will you take this week to respond to what God has already spoken?

Take your time with these reflections. Each one invites you to shift from simply believing God loves you to actually living as someone secure in that love. Refining does not reduce you. It reveals you. It calls out the daughter God always saw beneath the layers of fear, striving, and self-protection.

When the Father spoke identity over me, something settled in my spirit. His word did more than comfort me. It reshaped me. My thoughts slowed. My prayers deepened. My posture changed from performing for approval to resting in assurance. Distance gave way to closeness. Anxiety gave way to alignment. I finally understood that identity is not achieved. It is received.

The moment Heaven called me "daughter," every old label lost its authority. I no longer lived to earn worth. I lived from it. That revelation became the doorway to the next season, rebirth. What God spoke over me began to rewire how I moved, how I believed, and how I surrendered.

The chapter that follows reveals how identity became transformation. When God names you, He also renews you. Rebirth is where that renewal begins.

Closing Prayer

Father, thank You for calling me "daughter" when I had nothing to prove and everything to surrender. I release every false label, every need to perform, and every fear of rejection. I receive Your Spirit of adoption and the peace that comes with being Yours. Break every lie that tells me love must be earned. Heal the memories that shaped my striving and restore my confidence in Your grace. Let Your truth redefine how I see myself and how I love others. Teach me to rest in Your presence and to walk as a daughter who trusts her Father completely. Let this identity stay firm in my spirit and overflow into everything I do. In Jesus' name, **Amen.**

PART TWO: THE BECOMING

WHERE IDENTITY IS REDISCOVERED, AND HEALING BEGINS.

Chapter 5
THE SECOND BIRTH

R ebirth at forty-five did not make me late; it made me honest. For decades, I had been running, performing, and pretending I was fine. I had walked through marriage, motherhood, heartbreak, and church life while still carrying the weight of unhealed pain. Then came a quiet night when everything fell still. There was no worship team, no pastor, no altar call, just me on my knees, asking God for mercy.

Liquid prayers replaced words. Every regret, every broken promise, every failed attempt at control poured out through those tears. I had spent years trying to earn what had already been given, grace, love, and belonging. That night, I finally received them. Relief came first, then peace, and then a strange kind of joy that had no performance attached to it.

Memoir Moments

The old Josette died quietly. There was no applause, only the sound of surrender. What began as repentance became renewal. That moment was not dramatic, but it was sacred. It felt like coming home.

Homecoming at 45 (Born Again)

It happened in quiet surrender. I was forty-five, and the room was still. No music played, no one was watching, and there was nothing left to prove. The weight of years pressed on me, years of striving, heartbreak, and pretending strength, but that night, I could not carry it any longer. I fell to my knees and began to weep. My words came out as broken whispers, asking God to have mercy, to help me, to take over where I had failed.

It was not a dramatic scene, just a woman reaching the end of herself. I cried until my body felt emptied of everything false. Those tears were not weakness; they were release. It felt like layers were being peeled away, one by one, until my heart could breathe again. My spirit quieted, and the only thing I could sense was peace.

The old Josette died quietly that night. There was no applause, no audience, only the sound of surrender and the presence of a God who had been waiting all along. I could feel His mercy in the silence. The scales on my eyes began to lift, and I could see with a new kind of clarity.

I realized that this was not about earning love anymore. I wasn't performing for love anymore; I was receiving it. The striving stopped. The shame faded. For the first time, I felt safe in His presence, not judged, not disqualified, just loved. It was the night heaven called me home, and I finally said yes.

Grief & Gratitude

Grief met me before language did. Long before I learned how to pray with confidence, my healing began in silence. When surrender came at forty-five, my tears did not sound like the ones I had cried in earlier seasons. These were different. They were not the frantic sobs of a woman trying to find God; they were the steady release of someone finally letting Him in.

I sat on the floor and felt years uncurl inside me. Memories surfaced without warning. I remembered the versions of myself I had abandoned to survive. I remembered the moments I had chosen strength because softness felt too dangerous. The tears that fell were not frantic; they were cleansing. They washed away the noise, the pressure, and the masks I had worn for decades.

This time, I was not weeping over people or past decisions. I was grieving the places in me that had never known safety, and at the same time, I was grateful that God had waited for me. Grief and gratitude kept taking turns in my chest. One breath released pain, the next welcomed mercy. I realized that these tears were not a breakdown, they were evidence that something new was forming.

When the weeping finally slowed, the room felt different. My breathing steadied, my thoughts settled, and peace rose quietly like dawn. It was not loud or dramatic. It simply took its place; the way light enters a room when the curtains finally open.

Those tears were my surrender. The peace that followed was His response.

Spiritual Clarity & Daily Rhythms

After being born again, my days began to change. Mornings became sacred. I would open my Bible before sunrise, the pages spread across the table, my phone on silent. The quiet felt full, as if heaven was already awake and waiting. I prayed simple prayers, honest, direct, without pretense. Worship followed, not loud but steady, a whisper of thanksgiving that filled my small space.

Fasting became my act of consecration. It was no longer about skipping meals; it was about silencing the noise that kept me from hearing God. I learned that fasting was a posture of surrender, a way to tune my heart to His voice. During those hours, clarity would come like light breaking through fog.

A year later, I received the gift of tongues. It was not dramatic; it was divine. The Holy Spirit-filled language flowed like a secret conversation between my spirit and God. My prayer room shifted that day. It no longer felt like I was talking to Him; it felt like I was communing with Him. And in that stillness, clarity became my constant companion.

Community Resistance, Isolation & Vocation (Spa Owner)

After being born again, not everyone understood the change. Some around me thought I had become too intense, too spiritual, too serious about the things of God. What they saw as extreme was really my hunger for truth. Their misunderstanding did not offend me; it revealed how deep the transformation had gone. I learned to be content with solitude, trusting that God was doing something in private that no one else could yet see.

During that same season, my work at the spa became a sacred assignment. Serving others through self-care mirrored what God was doing within me. Each client who sat in my chair became a reminder that healing takes gentleness, patience, and presence. As I anointed others with oils and words of encouragement, I felt the Holy Spirit anointing me with peace and stability. My hands were serving, but my heart was being restored.

While hands were anointing others, God was steadying mine.

Holy Fire & Identity Shift

Over time, a steady fire began to grow inside me. It was not loud or wild, but consistent and holy. The more I prayed, fasted, and spent time in God's presence, the more my desires changed. What once tempted me lost its pull. The boundaries I once resisted became my protection. Purity was no longer pressure; it became peace.

Conviction came quickly, but so did forgiveness. I started to guard my thoughts and words, not out of fear but from love. Every decision began to flow from a place of clarity. I could sense the Holy Spirit shaping my responses, teaching me when to speak, when to wait, and when to release. The change was not forced, it was the evidence of new life.

I wasn't trying to be new; I had become new.

Devotional Insight

Born Again: John 3:3–8

"Jesus replied, 'Very truly I tell you, no one can see the kingdom of God unless they are born again.'"

Rebirth is not something achieved through effort. It is Spirit-born, not self-willed. My second birth at forty-five was not the result of striving harder but of surrendering fully. In that quiet moment of repentance, God breathed new life into me. What years of performance could not produce, one encounter with His Spirit made complete. I realized salvation is not earned through works; it is received through faith.

New Creation: 2 Corinthians 5:17

"Therefore, if anyone is in Christ, the new creation has come: The old has gone, the new is here."

When I rose from that place of surrender, I felt peace cover me like a garment. The old Josette, the one tied to shame, fear, and striving, was gone. I did not need a new name to prove it; the evidence was in my peace. This verse became the mirror that reminded me I was no longer defined by my past but redefined by His presence.

Washing & Renewal: Titus 3:5

"He saved us, not because of righteous things we had done, but because of His mercy. He saved us through the washing of rebirth and renewal by the Holy Spirit."

The Lord taught me that true deliverance is not about managing sin but submitting to cleansing. Every fast, every tear, every prayer became a rinse of the heart. It was not about proving holiness; it was about allowing the Holy Spirit to do what only He could, purify me from within. The more I surrendered, the freer I became.

God Restores Time: Joel 2:25

"I will restore to you the years that the locust has eaten."

When I looked back on decades of mistakes and missed opportunities, I feared it was too late. But God reminded me that time belongs to Him. What was lost in disobedience, He can multiply in obedience. My rebirth at forty-five was not delayed; it was divine timing. He gave me back what I thought I had forfeited, purpose, hope, and a clean slate.

For You: God restores what you release. Trust Him with your wasted years; He knows how to redeem everyone.

The Shepherd's Provision: Psalm 23:1

"The Lord is my shepherd; I shall not want."

After my rebirth, peace became my daily provision. I stopped searching for fulfillment in people, titles, or possessions. The more I let Him lead, the less I lacked. Even in quiet seasons, I sensed His presence feeding my spirit. Contentment was no longer a theory; it became proof that I trusted Him.

A New Thing: Isaiah 43:19

"See, I am doing a new thing! Now it springs up; do you not perceive it?"

The Lord began to open my perception through fasting, prayer, and the gift of tongues. Each discipline was not a ritual but a channel of grace. Fasting tuned my heart to hear Him clearly. Speaking in tongues brought intimacy that words could not express. Deliverance removed what blocked my vision. Through these acts of obedience, I saw new life springing up all around me.

For You

Where are you still trying to earn what God already gave freely?

What simple rhythm; Word, worship, or fasting will you begin this week to strengthen your relationship with Him?

Let these truths settle deep within you:

- You are not performing for love; you are receiving it.

- Your past is not your identity; Christ defines you.

- Purity grows through surrender, not striving.

- Time is not lost when placed in God's hands.

- Peace becomes provision when He leads.

- Something new is rising within you, even if it feels hidden.

New beginnings do not wait for perfect conditions.

They begin the moment you say yes.

The Refining Room (Interactive Encounter)

Prophetic Declarations

- I am a new creation; the old has passed.

- I trade striving for sonship and performance for presence.

- My tears have spoken; my Shepherd has answered.

- Fasting tunes my ear, and the Spirit strengthens my will.

- My prayer language unlocks intimacy and intercession.

- Generational curses break: blessings begin with me.

- What I lost in years, God restores in purpose.

Journal Prompts

1. If you stopped performing for God for one week, what would pursuing His presence look like instead? Name one concrete change you can make today.

2. Which rhythm will you start or strengthen this week; Scripture at dawn, a weekly fast, or ten-minute tongues walk? Choose one and set a specific time for it.

3. Write a one-sentence decree over your bloodline. Example: "As for me and my house, we will serve the Lord; cycles end with me."

Take time with these reflections. Let them shape your next act of obedience. Refining is not punishment; it is preparation for restoration.

It felt like coming home. Every prayer, every tear, and every act of surrender brought me closer to the peace I had searched for my entire life. Being born again at forty-five did not make me late; it made me ready. Ready to live without masks. Ready to serve God with a clean heart. Ready to believe that new beginnings are not bound by age but by obedience.

This second birth reintroduced me to life as God intended it; anchored in truth, shaped by grace, and sustained by His presence. The woman who once chased healing now walks in wholeness. The one who once lived for approval now rests in acceptance.

New birth begs new boundaries. In the next chapter, I will share how holiness became my protection, not my punishment.

Closing Prayer

Father, thank You for meeting me in a quiet room and calling me home. I receive the washing of renewal and the Spirit of adoption. Cleanse what I cannot fix, reorder what I cannot manage, and set my heart to Your rhythms of Word, worship, fasting, and obedience. Baptize my prayers with Your power and let my tears water new life. Restore the years the locusts have eaten and anchor my family in Your covenant love. Teach me to walk in peace, to trust Your voice above all others, and to remain steady in Your will. I choose Your presence over performance and Your truth over emotion. In Jesus' name, **Amen.**

Chapter 6

SET APART FOR SOMETHING SACRED

Purity didn't begin as a rule for me, it arrived as revelation. After my deliverance and rebirth, I finally understood that God had not been punishing me by removing certain people or desires. He was protecting me. What I once called restriction was actually preservation. Every "no" that felt painful was a shield keeping me from returning to what He already freed me from.

When counterfeit love ended, the covenant began. Purity became more than a lifestyle; it became a language of devotion. It was how I told God, *"You can trust me now."* My obedience became worship, and boundaries became love letters written back to the One who had rescued me.

This new season was not about rules or repression. It was about reverence. Purity became the evidence that I had been made whole a reflection of honor, integrity, and surrender. I learned that holiness was never meant to cage me; it was meant to cover me.

This is how God set me apart for something sacred.

Memoir Moments

Purity: Revelation → Covenant

After my deliverance, I realized purity had never been about restriction. It was protection. God was not punishing me by separating me from what I once thought I needed. He was teaching me that peace requires distance from anything counterfeit. For the first time, I understood that purity was His way of keeping me safe while He rebuilt me.

I had given pieces of myself to people who never covered me in prayer. They liked my strength but could not handle my spirit. I had confused attention for love and validation for value. When God delivered me, He made it clear that the next season would require consecration. I could not expect divine alignment while living in divided loyalty. Purity became my protection plan.

Obedience became my love language. Each "yes" to God and "no" to temptation was my way of saying, *I trust you more than I trust my feelings.* Purity was not performance, it was partnership. It reminded me that real intimacy with God required boundaries, reverence, and self-control.

I also learned to define what purity meant in my own life. Celibacy is a vow of lifelong singleness devoted to serving God fully. Abstinence is choosing to wait for covenant before sharing physical intimacy. But purity is deeper, it is whole-life consecration. It shapes how I think, how I speak, and how I treat others. It affects what I watch, who I listen to, and how I manage my emotions.

This understanding changed everything. Purity was not a loophole or a substitute for legalism. It was a covenant, a sacred promise between me and God that I would honor Him with my body, my thoughts, and my relationships.

Purity wasn't a loophole; it was a covenant.

Purity Beyond Sex (Consecration)

Purity became more than a choice to abstain from sex; it became a way of life. It was no longer about behavior but about becoming. Purity meant worship. It meant fasting when distractions tried to cloud my discernment. It meant prayer when emotions wanted to lead. It meant repentance when pride tried to return. Every act of obedience became sacred. Every boundary became an altar.

Purity shaped what I consumed and what I cultivated. It taught me to guard what entered through my eyes and ears. Music, conversations, and media were no longer harmless entertainment; they were influences that either fed my spirit or drained it. I learned that purity required discipline in private, not just presentation in public. It was about who I was when no one was watching.

My days began with the Word, continued with worship, and ended with accountability. This rhythm kept me grounded and aware. When temptation whispered, truth spoke louder. When loneliness tried to settle in, prayer filled the space.

People often said, "You're just abstaining," but I knew it was more than that. Abstinence is waiting. Consecration is living set apart. Purity for me was not about deprivation; it was about dedication. It was not a pause before marriage but a practice of holiness that touched every area of life.

I was not just abstaining. It was consecration.

Loneliness and Temptation → Devotion

Loneliness became my teacher. It showed me where I had filled space with noise instead of presence. When the crowds disappeared and the phone stopped ringing, I discovered that solitude was not punishment. It was an invitation. God was teaching me to run to devotion instead of distraction.

My days became structured around quiet communion. I played worship music softly in the mornings as I journaled what the Holy Spirit revealed during prayer. I went on long walks, speaking in tongues under my breath, allowing peace to rise where anxiety once lived. My phone stayed on "Do Not Disturb," not because I wanted isolation but because I wanted intimacy with God.

Temptation still came, but so did conviction. Whenever an old pattern tried to return, I remembered the freedom I had fought for and the cost of my deliverance. The thought of losing that peace reminded me why purity mattered. When I fell short in thought or attitude, I repented quickly. Repentance was no longer shame-driven; it was love-driven.

Accountability kept me grounded. I surrounded myself with believers who valued truth over comfort and prayer over gossip. Their honesty reminded me that holiness was not a solo pursuit.

Loneliness taught me to worship before I worried, to pray before I reacted, and to seek God before seeking comfort elsewhere. I stopped fearing silence and started to find God in it.

Instead of filling the silence, I let worship fill me.

Set-Apart Rhythms (Everyday Life)

Being set apart was not about grand gestures. It showed up in small, consistent choices. Modesty shaped how I dressed and spoke. Integrity guided my private actions when no one was watching. I guarded my conversations, steering away from gossip and negativity, and I watched what I allowed into my mind through media and music. What I consumed became a reflection of what I valued.

At home and at work, I learned to live my faith transparently. As a school leader, I carried my beliefs quietly but firmly. My tone, patience, and compassion were my testimony. I did not have to announce my calling; I simply lived it.

Obedience often meant saying no to opportunities that seemed appealing but lacked divine purpose. I turned down what was popular to protect what was prophetic. It was not perfection but pursuit. The fruit of the Spirit began to show in my words, my leadership, and my ability to love with grace.

Being set apart became my rhythm of worship. Every decision was a seed of obedience, and every boundary was a sign of growth.

The Hardest Boundary (Emotional)

The hardest boundary to enforce was emotional. Letting go of people I cared for deeply required more courage than fasting or prayer. It meant blocking numbers, closing doors gracefully, and obeying the quiet voice of the Holy Spirit. Some connections were comforting but not covenant. God showed me that alignment mattered more than attachment.

There was an almost partnership that looked promising, even ministry focused. It was a good idea, but not a God idea. The Lord removed it before it could take root, and I thanked Him later. Each act of obedience became another step toward wholeness.

My peace came when I stopped fighting to keep what God was releasing. I learned that detachment was not cruelty; it was clarity.

I chose obedience over attachment, even when my feelings disagreed.

Devotional Insight

God's Will: Sanctification — 1 Thessalonians 4:3–5

"It is God's will that you should be sanctified: that you should avoid sexual immorality; that each of you should learn to control your own body in a way that is holy and honorable."

Purity is not just preference; it is purpose. God's will for every believer is sanctification, which means being set apart for Him. Holiness does not rob you of joy; it restores your design. When I understood this, I stopped seeing purity as denial and started seeing it as direction. God was not taking something from me; He was preparing me for something greater. Purity protected my destiny and healed my desires.

Temple Theology — 1 Corinthians 6:18–20

"Do you not know that your bodies are temples of the Holy Spirit, who is in you, whom you have received from God? You are not your own; you were bought at a price. Therefore, honor God with your bodies."

When I realized my body was a temple, not a tool, everything changed. My body was not leverage for attention or acceptance; it was God's dwelling place. Purity became worship, not willpower. Honoring God with my body meant treating it as sacred ground where His Spirit lives. It meant that self-control was not about repression but reverence.

Guard the Wellspring — Proverbs 4:23

"Above all else, guard your heart, for everything you do flows from it."

Boundaries for your eyes and ears are not legalism; they are mercy. What enters your senses will eventually shape your soul. Guarding my heart meant filtering what I watched, listened to, and allowed into my space. God showed me that discipline was not meant to control me but to keep me clean. A guarded heart became a peaceful heart, and peace produced clarity.

Blessed Are the Pure — Matthew 5:8

"Blessed are the pure in heart, for they will see God."

Purity sharpens spiritual vision. When my motives were cleansed, I began to discern God's presence in everyday moments. I could see His hand in decisions, conversations, and divine interruptions. Purity cleared the fog of confusion that sin once caused. The more I obeyed, the clearer His guidance became.

Living Sacrifice — Romans 12:1–2

"Therefore, I urge you, brothers and sisters, in view of God's mercy, to offer your bodies as a living sacrifice, holy and pleasing to God; this is your true and proper worship."

Purity begins in the mind. Transformation is not about trying harder but thinking differently. When my thoughts aligned with God's truth, my actions followed. I learned that surrendering my body without renewing my mind created cycles of struggle. Renewal broke them. Purity became less about behavior and more about identity, living as someone already loved and chosen.

Resist and replace— James 4:7

"Submit yourselves, then, to God. Resist the devil, and he will flee from you."

Resistance only works when it is paired with replacement. When I resisted temptation, I also filled the space with worship, Scripture, or prayer. God did not just remove counterfeits; He replaced them with His presence.

Every temptation became an opportunity to strengthen my obedience. The same God who delivered me also trained me to stay free.

Fruit Over Fireworks — Galatians 5:22–23

"But the fruit of the Spirit is love, joy, peace, forbearance, kindness, goodness, faithfulness, gentleness and self-control."

The true proof of purity is not perfection; it is fruit. Gentleness replaced defensiveness. Self-control replaced indulgence. Love replaced fear. The more I yielded to the Spirit, the more fruit grew naturally. Fireworks draw attention, but fruit sustains transformation. I stopped measuring purity by how well I resisted sin and started measuring it by how consistently I reflected Christ.

For You

Ask the Holy Spirit to reveal one area where He is calling you to deeper purity.

Replace one daily distraction with a time of prayer or Scripture.

Choose fruit over feelings, obedience over impulse, and holiness over haste.

Purity is not the absence of desire; it is the alignment of desire with the heart of God.

The Refining Room (Interactive Encounter)

This is the moment where reflection becomes renewal. The words you speak and the prayers you release will seal the covenant that purity started. Speak each declaration with intention. Let your voice carry agreement with heaven.

Prophetic Declarations

- Purity is my covenant, not my punishment.

- I choose obedience over entanglement.

- My mind, mouth, and media are consecrated.

- I turn down what is popular to protect what is prophetic.

- Loneliness becomes intimacy; temptation becomes testimony.

- I set emotional boundaries and keep spiritual access holy.

- I am set apart for something sacred.

Journal Prompts

1. When loneliness tries to return, what devotional rhythm will you choose instead? Commit to ten minutes this week in worship, journaling, reading Scripture, or praying in tongues. Schedule it as an act of love, not obligation.

2. Identify three emotional or relational boundaries you must protect this month. For each, write the exact sentence you will use if that boundary is tested. This clarity keeps your obedience steady when emotions rise.

3. Choose one media habit that weakens your purity and replace it with a Scripture to meditate on instead. Let the Word become your soundtrack and your safeguard.

Purity is how I say "I love You" back. It is not a cage; it is a covering. Every no I give the world is a yes, I give to God. Being set apart did not shrink my life; it safeguarded my promise.

This chapter was never about perfection, it was about alignment. Consecration taught me to choose presence over pressure and peace over performance. What once felt like isolation became intimacy.

The next chapter reveals what happened in that hidden place. Consecration prepared me for the waiting room, where oil is formed in the secret place.

Closing Prayer

Father, thank You for revealing purity as protection and covenant. I surrender my thoughts, my words, my habits, and my desires to You. Teach me to love You with my boundaries and honor You with my body. Guard my eyes and ears; reorder my appetites; make my home and my work holy ground. Where I have been entangled, untie me. Where I have been lonely, meet me. Where I have been tempted, strengthen me. I choose obedience over attachment and presence over popularity. Set me apart for something sacred. In Jesus' name, **Amen.**

PART THREE: THE REFINING

WHERE PAIN BECOMES POWER AND OBEDIENCE
BIRTHS OVERFLOW.

Chapter 7

HEALED IN THE HIDDEN PLACE

God met me where I least expected, in the waiting room. It was not in a revival service, not in a crowd, but under fluorescent hospital lights with my heart full of fear and my hands trembling. That is where peace found me.

Memoir Moments

The diagnosis arrived without warning and the walls began to close in. Machines hummed louder than my thoughts. There were questions I could not answer, results I could not control, and prayers that escaped through tears instead of words. I sat between uncertainty and surrender, trying to steady my breath.

Those sterile rooms became sanctuaries. Every delay forced me to listen. Every doctor's report pushed me closer to the only Physician who never misdiagnoses. I learned that healing is not always immediate, it can be a holy process that exposes what silence conceals.

God was not absent from the MRI table. He was present in the stillness, working through it. What began as pressure became purpose. What looked like illness became an invitation. My pain became the altar where God performed surgery on my soul.

This is how hidden illness became my healing classroom. The waiting room was never wasted. It was where God refined my faith, restored my peace, and prepared me for the oil that only forms in secret.

Hidden Illness & Early Hypertension

I was in my early thirties when the blood pressure numbers started to rise. The doctor's office always felt colder than it should have, and the waiting room was filled with elderly patients clutching pill organizers and walking canes. I sat among them, pretending to scroll through my phone, quietly embarrassed that my name belonged on the same sign in chart. Their conversations about cholesterol and medication made me feel out of place, too young to belong there yet too weary to argue with the diagnosis.

The prescriptions came one after another, new combinations, adjusted dosages, hopeful follow-ups. Each appointment carried the same question in my heart: *When will this end?* I told myself I was close to healing every time a reading improved, only to face another setback. It became a pattern of almost, but not quite. My blood pressure would stabilize for a few months, then climb again as if my body refused to cooperate with my prayers.

Behind the polite smiles and quiet compliance, I carried frustration that few saw. I wanted to live free from the labels written in red ink on my file. I wanted to stop feeling older than I was. Looking back, I now see that this was only the beginning. There was a deeper story waiting beneath the numbers, a lesson about surrender, not control.

I felt too young for the charts, and too tired for the fight.

3:00 a.m. Wakeups & Stirring of Calling

After being born again, the quiet hours before dawn began to stir something unfamiliar yet holy inside me. Almost every night, I found myself waking up around three or four in the morning, wide awake for no obvious reason. At first, I blamed anxiety or broken sleep patterns, but it kept happening. The same hour. The same pull. The same stillness that felt sacred even when I could not describe it.

One morning, caught between sleep and awareness, I whispered, "Lord... me?" The question carried both reverence and disbelief. I started researching why those hours kept calling me and I learned that God often wakes His chosen ones when the world grows silent. Nothing about it felt dramatic. It wasn't emotional. It was obedient.

As the months passed, I realized these awakenings were not disruptions; they were invitations. Waking up at 3 a.m. belongs to what many call the **Fourth Watch**—a prophetic hour marked by revelation, warfare, and heightened spiritual sensitivity. It is also known as **the Seer's time**, a window where Heaven feels near and the veil between the natural and the spiritual grows thin.

I often felt a sudden quickening in my spirit, a holy awareness sweeping the room. The air would settle, the atmosphere would shift, and I sensed the Lord's presence drawing me to prayer. Sometimes it felt as though angels were standing guard, creating a covering for whatever God wanted to reveal. It was not fear. It was reverence.

This is also the hour many believe Jesus faced the weight of crucifixion, the hour of surrender, sacrifice, and victory. With every awakening, I understood more clearly that God was not interrupting my sleep; He was initiating my training. Before illness touched my natural eyes, He was sharpening my spiritual sight. Before anyone affirmed the prophetic call on my life, He was already awakening the Seer within me.

Those early hours became my private altar. The house was dark, the world still, yet His presence felt alive and close. I realized I was not waking up because of restlessness; I was waking up because of purpose. God was drawing me into a hidden classroom, a protected place where obedience taught me what understanding could not. Long before I knew I carried a mantle; Heaven was preparing me for it.

Diagnosis: IIH, Swollen Optic Nerves, Tests

The diagnosis came after a chain of appointments that December. It began with my gynecologist, who found a small cyst on my left ovary. That alone was concerning, but I continued with my scheduled visits. My primary care doctor checked my blood pressure, still elevated but stable, and encouraged me to see an ophthalmologist after I mentioned new vision problems.

The visit that changed everything happened in that ophthalmologist's office. I expected to leave with a new prescription for glasses. Instead, I was told my optic nerves were swollen, a sign of Idiopathic Intracranial

Hypertension. The words hit me like a wave. I had never heard of the condition before. The doctor explained that it involved excess pressure around the brain and required further tests, MRIs, MRVs, and a neuro-ophthalmology consultation.

The fear set in immediately. I dreaded the MRI more than the results. The thought of lying in that closed tube made me feel trapped. My first attempt failed; I walked out before the machine even started. Later, I found a stand-up MRI facility and tried again, sitting upright this time, whispering prayers between the loud clicks. The images were usable but not perfect. The neuro-ophthalmologist confirmed what I feared, my optic nerves were severely swollen. She spoke of venograms and possible stenting procedures to relieve the pressure.

The process felt endless, the appointments overwhelming. Yet while my body faced physical confinement, my spirit was expanding. God was pressing into places I had not surrendered before. What looked like medical chaos became spiritual refinement.

When the machine enclosed me, God invited me to elevate in Him.

Isolation → Surrender → Intimacy

When the tests, appointments, and uncertainty became too heavy to manage, I reached the place where control no longer worked. I could not control my health, but I could surrender my heart. That decision changed everything.

Isolation became my new environment, yet it was not empty. It was filled with whispers from God that met me in silence. My prayers turned into tears, and those tears became my language. They were what I now call liquid prayers, moments when words failed, but my spirit still spoke. Every tear carried a plea and every sob felt understood.

Fasting became my rhythm. It was not about abstaining from food, but about silencing the noise. Stillness taught me lessons that busyness never could. I began to see that the hidden season was not punishment; it was purification. God was teaching me how to find Him in the quiet, how to sense His nearness in what seemed like abandonment.

The world outside slowed, but something holy awakened within me. That stillness turned into sacred intimacy. I gave Him everything I couldn't hold.

Small Miracles & Healing Progress

Healing did not come all at once. It came quietly, through small moments that felt ordinary but carried divine fingerprints. One morning, I opened my eyes and realized the pressure in my head had lessened. Another day, the blurriness faded faster than before. The redness in my eyes softened, and the headaches that once ruled my mornings began to release their grip.

Every small improvement felt like God's signature written across my body. Nurses offered kind words that carried peace. Scriptures appeared at just the right time, reminding me that healing was not instant, it was intimate. The Holy Spirit comforted me when fear tried to return, whispering that progress could be slow but still sacred.

I stopped measuring healing by the absence of pain and started recognizing it by the presence of peace. Healing began as peace long before it finished as proof.

Devotional Insight

The God Who Sees in Secret — Matthew 6:6

"When you pray, go into your room, close the door, and pray to your Father who is unseen. Then your Father, who sees what is done in secret, will reward you."

My secret place became my sanctuary. It was my prayer chair, my altar, my worship playlist, and my journal full of tears and gratitude. That space was where God met me without pretense. He did not need eloquence; He needed honesty. The Father who sees in secret shaped me in silence. When the world could not see progress, heaven was recording transformation.

Near to the Brokenhearted — Psalm 34:18

"The Lord is close to the brokenhearted and saves those who are crushed in spirit."

Liquid prayers became my offering. I had no words, only tears streaming down my face. Yet God heard every drop. He did not need paragraphs to understand pain. He translated weeping into worship and sorrow into surrender. His nearness wrapped around my grief like a blanket, reminding me that my brokenness was not a barrier but an invitation.

Do Not Fear, For I Am with You — Isaiah 41:10

"So do not fear, for I am with you; do not be dismayed, for I am your God."

Fear visited me often, in hospital waiting rooms, during MRIs, and while waiting for results. Yet through every test, God was steadying my breath. His presence did not erase fear instantly, but it quieted its control. I learned to name my fears out loud and invite His presence into them. Fear lost its grip when faith entered the conversation.

Peace Beyond Understanding — Philippians 4:6–7

"Do not be anxious about anything, but in every situation, by prayer and petition, with thanksgiving, present your requests to God."

Anxiety filled the spaces between test results and doctor calls. I prayed not for quick answers but for steady peace. As I practiced gratitude, I noticed my heart becoming guarded, not by denial, but by divine calm. Prayer did not always change circumstances immediately, but it always changed my posture. Peace became evidence that God was already working behind the scenes.

My Grace is Sufficient — 2 Corinthians 12:9

"My grace is sufficient for you, for my power is made perfect in weakness."

My body felt fragile, but His strength filled the gaps. Every weakness exposed His power. Healing was not instant, but it was intimate. I stopped praying for perfection and started thanking Him for grace. The same weakness that made me tremble became the doorway where His glory entered.

The Lord Who Heals You — Exodus 15:26; 1 Peter 2:24

"For I am the Lord who heals you."

Jehovah Rapha met me in every appointment. Healing came through both miracle and medicine, through both prayer and patience. Some days it was an improvement on the chart; other days it was the courage to get out of bed. He healed layer by layer, both body and soul. Healing was not a moment but a process.

Anointed in the Secret Place — Psalm 91:1; Psalm 23:5

"He who dwells in the secret place of the Most High shall abide under the shadow of the Almighty."

Oil forms in obscurity. Before platforms or public praise, God anoints in private. The hidden place became holy ground where I received new instructions and peace for what was ahead. I realized that intimacy with Him is the real anointing. The waiting room was not wasted; it was where oil formed.

For You

Where is God asking you to turn your waiting room into a worship room?

What would "intimate, not instant" change about your expectations this week?

How can you honor the hidden place as holy ground?

The Refining Room (Interactive Encounter)

The refining room is where faith meets reality. It is not filled with noise or crowds but with quiet surrender. This space allows the Holy Spirit to polish what pain revealed. Healing is not just recovery; it is refinement. Every test, diagnosis, and delay become a tool in the hands of a perfect Teacher. What once felt like pressure is transformed into preparation. Here, we learn to breathe again, to believe again, and to bow again.

When God brings us into a refining season, He removes the unnecessary so that what is eternal can remain. It is uncomfortable, yet holy. The silence that once felt heavy now feels sacred. The stillness that once felt empty now feels anointed. In this space, the fire does not consume, it purifies. What remains after the testing is stronger, clearer, and surrendered.

This is where the waiting room turns into worship and pain becomes prayer. The refining room is not punishment; it is the Father's embrace, shaping us to reflect His image. He is not just healing the body; He is healing how we see, how we trust, and how we respond. This is where the child of God becomes the vessel of purpose.

Prophetic Declarations

Read them slowly, letting each line settle in your spirit. Speak them aloud until your atmosphere agrees with your faith.

- My hidden place is holy ground.

- I trade panic for Presence and fear for faith.

- Healing may not be instant, but it is intimate.

- Peace is proof that God is here.

- By Jesus' stripes, I am healed in every layer.

- I receive fresh oil in the waiting room.

- What pressed me will not define me.

Journal Prompts

1. What small act can turn your waiting into worship this week? Choose one, reading a Psalm aloud, singing one worship song before bed, or spending five minutes in quiet gratitude. Write the specific time or place you will commit to it.

2. Identify three "small wins" that reminded you of God's nearness this week. It could be reduced pain, a verse that comforted you, or someone's unexpected kindness. Write how each one reveals His hand at work, even in small details.

3. Finish this statement honestly: "Lord, I cannot control *but I surrender* and receive Your peace." After writing it, read it out loud. Notice how peace follows confession.

These reflections are not about finding perfect answers but about locating peace. God meets you in honest words, whispered prayers, and quiet surrender. The waiting room becomes holy ground when your focus shifts from outcomes to intimacy with Him.

The hidden place became holy ground. What once felt like isolation revealed itself as intimacy. I learned that surrender was not the end of strength but the beginning of healing. My body was recovering, but more importantly, my faith was being refined. Every moment in silence became proof that God never left the room.

Healing did not start with a doctor's report; it began the day I released control. The waiting room turned into worship. The diagnosis became a doorway to deeper dependence. When I stopped fighting the process, I discovered peace waiting for me. My healing began when my surrender did.

Now I see that what felt like delay was really divine preparation. God was forming endurance, oil, and trust that would be needed for the next chapter of my calling. The waiting did not waste me; it refined me.

What didn't consume me clarified me. Next comes the chapter where the fire forged endurance and faith grew stronger through testing. The story continues, not with weakness, but with worship.

Closing Prayer

Father, thank You for meeting me in the refining room. When silence surrounded me, You were still speaking. When fear rose, Your peace remained. I surrender every diagnosis, delay, and disappointment to You. I yield to Your process and receive Your power.

Teach me to see pressure as preparation. Let Your refining fire remove doubt, pride, and fear. Replace every anxious thought with the certainty of Your love. Purify my motives and strengthen my mind. Let Your Spirit breathe fresh faith into my lungs.

I declare that my body, mind, and soul belong to You. I receive Your healing in every hidden place. Thank You for making my pain purposeful and my waiting fruitful. You are the God who restores, redeems, and renews. As I sit in stillness, let peace become my testimony. I am refined, not ruined. I am healed, not hindered. I am kept, called, and covered in Your love. In Jesus' name, **Amen**.

Chapter 8

FIRE-TESTED FAITH

The furnace found me in a year that would not let up. Heat from every side. Heart, body, resources. I call this my favorite chapter because the flame told the truth and God stayed.

Here is the thesis without polish. Fire exposes what flares, purifies what stays, and prepares what comes next. It did not finish me. It formed me. I walked through betrayal from a person I trusted in ministry and learned that blurred lines always burn. I faced a diagnosis that pressed behind my eyes and heard peace before I saw improvement. I woke to an empty curb where my car should have been and watched the Lord teach me order where zeal had run ahead of wisdom.

This chapter lays it out in scenes. First, the heart test that demanded boundaries and obedience. Then the body test that turned waiting rooms into worship rooms. Then the resource test that required repentance and a plan. One flame, three fronts, one testimony. The same God who let the heat rise held me steady inside it.

Turn the page. The fire did not consume me; it clarified me. And the gold He was after began to show.

Memoir Moments

Betrayal in Ministry (Emotional Fire)

I trusted someone in ministry who wore a warm smile and carried influence. We served, prayed, and planned together, and slowly the lines blurred. Compliments lingered past comfort. Conversations drifted from assignment to attention. Boundaries I once guarded began to feel negotiable because the setting felt holy. When the boundary finally broke, shock met grief. I had wanted partnership for purpose, yet my heart absorbed conflict and confusion. I sat with the Lord and named it plainly. This was compromise, not covenant.

The Holy Spirit had been whispering for weeks. I labeled it overthinking because ministry momentum looked fruitful. Then discernment burned bright. A quiet verse surfaced, first Peter one, verses six and seven, reminding me that trials refine faith. Psalm twenty-seven, verse thirteen, promised I would see the goodness of the Lord in the land of the living. I believed, and belief demanded action, even while emotions begged delay.

I drew a line and stepped back. I requested accountability for all future meetings, set public spaces, and ended private calls. I returned gifts, deleted threads, and released the need to explain what the Lord already exposed. The conversation that closed the door was brief, respectful, and firm. I blessed and released. That single act felt like leaving a smoky room for clean air. My body rested that night. My spirit matched my convictions.

The fire showed me where I had grown careless. I had spiritual language for compassion, yet no plan for guardrails. I had quick prayers, yet slow boundaries. I started listening sooner. I built clear expectations around time, touch, tone, and topics. I stayed accountable to trusted leaders and treated privacy as a privilege that required wisdom. I learned to leave when honor leaves the room. I chose the narrow way again, not to appear strong, but to stay submitted.

Looking back, I see grace in the exposure. First Peter 1:6–7 keeps my heart anchored, because refinement reveals what faith is truly made of. Psalm 27:13 continues to lift my focus, because God's goodness still meets me in the land of the living. I refuse to rewrite what God already revealed. I refuse to confuse attention with assignment. I will guard the call that guards my heart. The fire exposed weak places, uncovered red flags, and taught me that obedience is its own protection.

What the Fire Taught
(Boundaries, Obedience, Humility)

Fire taught me more than comfort ever could. It stripped my excuses and revealed what God required for me to mature in faith and leadership. Through pain, I gained clarity. Through surrender, I gained strength. These are the lessons that remain:

- **Clearer Boundaries:** I learned that protection is wisdom, not walls. Every boundary I ignored became an entry point for confusion. Guarding time, conversations, and emotional energy is now an act of obedience, not fear.

- **Faster Repentance:** I stopped delaying conviction. When correction came, I turned quickly. Delay always increases damage.

- **Humility Over Vindication:** Fire burned away the need to prove myself. God fought battles I never had to explain. I learned to stay silent and let integrity speak. Humility became my defense.

- **Discernment Over Desire:** I stopped calling comfort confirmation. I waited for peace, not popularity. Every major redirection required choosing God's approval over applause.

These lessons rewired my posture toward ministry and maturity. The Lord showed me that refinement begins where pride ends. The fire simplified my motives and steadied my focus. I stopped proving my worth and started protecting my assignment.

Medical Furnace: IIH & the Pressure Within

The diagnosis did not arrive through one dramatic moment. It crept in quietly, disguised as blurred morning vision and headaches I kept trying to explain away. I told myself it was stress, fatigue, maybe poor sleep. But each day, the fog lasted longer. My sight dimmed, returned, then dimmed again. It was a warning I could no longer ignore.

I moved from appointment to appointment, hoping someone would give me a simple explanation. A gynecologist found a small cyst. My primary doctor checked my numbers and suggested more tests. It was the ophthalmologist who finally paused, looked closer, and spoke the words that shifted everything: swollen optic nerves. Suspected Idiopathic Intracranial Hypertension. Pressure around the brain.

Nothing about it felt real at first. I had never heard of the condition. I did not know what it meant for my sight, my health, or my future. But the weight of the doctor's tone told me it mattered.

What followed felt like a medical marathon, MRIs, MRVs, dilation drops, bright machines, long hallways, technicians speaking in calm tones while my heart raced in my chest. The first MRI felt impossible. The walls of the tube pressed in before the machine even started. I walked out. Tears burned more than the fear itself. Later, I found a stand-up MRI and tried again. I prayed through every clank and vibration.

The neuro-ophthalmologist reviewed the images with a seriousness that made my body tense. The swelling was significant. She spoke of venograms, monitoring, and the possibility of stents. Every sentence felt heavier than the last. My head held pressure, but my heart held more.

Yet this chapter carried a different type of furnace. Chapter 7 was about hidden healing in quiet rooms. This moment was about heat, internal, relentless, and exposing. I was not just afraid; I was confronted. My faith, my peace, and my trust were being tested under pressure I could not escape.

I prayed in exam rooms. I prayed in elevators. I prayed in the car with my forehead against the steering wheel. I did not pray for perfection; I prayed for presence. And God met me differently here, not in whispers, but in stability. Not in goosebumps, but in grounding.

Headaches loosened. Vision steadied. The swelling began to ease. No sudden miracle, just slow mercy. Peace held me before answers did. And I realized healing sometimes comes like this, layered, gradual, measured by progress, not drama.

This furnace did not consume me; it clarified me.

It showed me that strength is not the absence of fear, but the decision to keep breathing while fear tries to close in.

It taught me that pressure does not break a woman God is training, it shapes her.

And in that shaping, I learned this truth:

Wholeness is not proven in scans; it is revealed in surrender.

Financial Furnace: Restoration & Repentance

The financial fire came quietly, hidden beneath good intentions and misplaced priorities. I had taken a consolidated loan that bundled my vehicle and a business loan for the spa I owned. The idea seemed practical at the time, one payment instead of two. Months later, an unpaid medical leave slowed my income, and the bills began to stack. I kept sowing into ministries, believing I was honoring God, but the Holy Spirit began to convict me. I was giving everywhere except where I owed. My zeal had outrun my stewardship.

One morning, I stepped outside for work and froze. The driveway stared back at me, bare and still. For a few seconds, I told myself I must have been mistaken, that everything was fine. Then reality settled like a heavy fog. The bank had already warned me that if I didn't make good on what I owed, there would be consequences. My heart sank, not just from the weight of financial strain, but from realizing how far I'd drifted from obedience. Yet even in that moment, faith began to rise to the surface. I stood on the curb and said aloud, "Lord, You are still in control." The words felt fragile, but I meant them, and they marked the beginning of repentance and the road toward recompense.

The shock pushed me into prayer and repentance. I realized obedience is not divided. Giving without managing what God already entrusted is partial obedience. I had been faithful in sowing but careless in structure. I opened my Bible to Proverbs chapter three, verses five and six. "Trust in the Lord with all your heart and lean not on your own understanding; in all your ways acknowledge Him, and He will make your paths straight." I wrote those words on a sticky note and placed it beside my laptop as a daily reminder.

Faith demanded more than tears. I set a deadline in faith and declared that every outstanding balance would be cleared before the end of the week. I made calls, rearranged priorities, and created a simple repayment plan. Every number I faced became a prayer point. I trusted God for supernatural favor, but I also learned to pick up the phone and face the debt directly. Repentance looked like responsibility.

By the end of that week, the payment was complete. The debt was cleared, and the vehicle was released. When I picked up the vehicle, gratitude flooded me. Joel chapter two, verse twenty-five, whispered through my mind: "I will restore to you the years that the locust has eaten." God restored what my disobedience had risked. I felt His mercy in motion.

That experience became a financial awakening. I began to track expenses, pray before purchases, and steward with understanding. I learned that faith without order creates cycles, not progress. Genesis chapter fifty, verse twenty, summarized the lesson perfectly: what the enemy meant for shame, God turned into testimony. The fire of loss exposed financial disorder and produced obedience and order. What once felt like failure became proof of refinement. Breakthrough followed repentance.

Breaking Point → Endurance
(Worship in the Ashes)

The hardest yes came when I had to walk away from someone I loved deeply. It was not a lack of emotion that pushed the decision, but obedience. I had to choose between comfort and calling. Every part of me wanted to stay, but peace had already left the room. God asked for surrender, and I finally gave Him what I had been holding back. Real faith holds God, not outcomes.

The days that followed were quiet and raw. My secret place became a sanctuary of tears, silence, and short prayers that barely formed into sentences. I stopped trying to sound strong and simply sat still. The Holy Spirit met me there. I learned that endurance is not white knuckling through pain. Endurance is worshiping while it still hurts. It is choosing reverence when reasoning fails.

Hebrews chapter eleven, verse one, defined the season: "Now faith is the substance of things hoped for, the evidence of things not seen." My eyes saw loss, but my spirit saw preparation. Isaiah chapter forty-one, verse ten, whispered courage: "Fear not, for I am with you; be not dismayed, for I am your God." Each verse became an anchor that kept me from sinking.

Endurance reshaped my strength. It taught me to rest inside trust, not to strive for control. Every sigh was worship, every tear a seed of belief that God would redeem what obedience cost. The breaking point became the birthplace of resilience. I learned to praise God not because I understood everything, but because I trusted His intentions toward me. Endurance became the quiet song of faith still standing in the ashes.

What Burned Away
(Things God Never Meant You to Carry)

The fire removed what I had once called strength but was really survival. It burned through idols of image and approval. People-pleasing disguised as humility disappeared in the heat. The need to control outcomes, to manage perception, and to perfect every detail turned to ash. God was not cruel in the process; He was thorough. He allowed me to see how much of my identity depended on roles, relationships, and recognition.

When the flames settled, the titles were gone, but peace remained. I realized that I had confused assignments with identity. God never asked me to carry every expectation or every outcome. He wanted my dependence, not my performance. Every false layer peeled away until only faith remained.

Isaiah chapter sixty-one, verse three, became a living reality: "To give them beauty for ashes, the oil of joy for mourning, the garment of praise for the spirit of heaviness." My ashes were not proof of failure; they were evidence of refining. Beauty rose from places that once carried regret.

What survived the fire was trust, not talent. Childlike dependence took the place of striving. My prayers grew simpler and my worship more sincere. I no longer reached for applause; I reached for alignment. God rebuilt me lighter and freer than before. The things that burned away made room for the things that truly matter.

Rebuilding from Ruins
(Personal Prophecy)

Isaiah chapter sixty-one, verse four, became my personal prophecy. It says, "They shall rebuild the old ruins, they shall raise up the former desolations, and they shall repair the ruined cities." Those words spoke directly into the places I thought were lost forever. Every heartbreak, diagnosis, and detour became a brick in my testimony. What once felt like scattered pieces began to align into purpose. The ruins were not wasted; they were repurposed.

God rebuilt my heart where betrayal had left cracks. He restored my reputation after seasons of misunderstanding. He stabilized my health, teaching me rest as a form of worship. He rebuilt my faith posture, not on emotion but on endurance. Every area touched by loss became a platform for His glory. Where I saw ashes, I now see oil. What once broke me now anoints me.

Psalm twenty-three, verse five, came alive in my spirit: "You prepare a table before me in the presence of my enemies; You anoint my head with oil; my cup runs over." The table was not revenge; it was restoration. The oil symbolized overflow, not excess. God took what was meant to humiliate and turned it into honor.

Rebuilding did not happen overnight. It came brick by brick, prayer by prayer. God did not erase the ruins; He built upon them. Every scar became a signature of grace. Every loss became an altar of gratitude. The prophecy fulfilled itself in daily obedience. What was once rubble became revelation. The fire that threatened to consume me became the very flame that illuminated my restoration.

Devotional Insight

The Refiner's Fire: Malachi 3:2–3

"He will sit as a refiner and purifier of silver; He will purify the Levites and refine them like gold and silver."

The fire does not come to punish you; it comes to prepare you. Malachi describes God as the Refiner who sits with intentional stillness, watching the silver until His reflection becomes clear. Refinement is not rushed. The heat exposes impurities that hinder holiness and reveals what faith often hides. God does not scorch; He skims. He removes what does not belong so that what remains can shine with purpose.

Trials that Mature Us: James 1:2–4

"Consider it pure joy whenever you face trials... because the testing of your faith produces perseverance... so that you may be mature and complete."

Your part in refinement is surrender. Trials are not signs of abandonment; they are invitations to maturity. Surrender is not passive. It is the courageous choice to tell the truth about what hurts and to trust that God will not waste an ounce of pain. Refinement is the cooperation of your honesty and His grace.

Hope Formed Through Pressure: Romans 5:3–5

"Suffering produces perseverance, perseverance, character, and character hope... and hope does not put us to shame."

When refinement exposes something painful, God is not condemning you. He is clarifying you. He burns away pride to reveal purity, dismantles false strength so true dependence can grow, and turns your desire for control into deeper trust. Every exposure is an expression of His love. His process is slow but steady, not rushed but purposeful.

Purified for Purpose: 1 Peter 1:6–7

"These trials will show that your faith is genuine. It is being tested as fire tests and purifies gold."

If you feel like you are standing in a furnace, do not run from the heat. Ask what it is refining, not who caused it. The fire you feel is not sent to destroy you; it is sent to distinguish you. Gold shines because it endured. So will you.

For You

If you are in a season of pressure or pruning, remember this truth: refinement is not rejection. God is making you radiant, not ruined. Release the urge to escape the heat and ask the Holy Spirit what He is revealing. Trust that every flame has purpose, and every test is shaping you for glory. The Refiner sees you, stays with you, and will finish what He began.

Fire exposes, but grace rebuilds. The same God who allows pressure also provides peace. When you surrender to His process, you discover that refinement is not loss. It is preparation for the oil that follows.

The Refining Room (Interactive Encounter)

Prophetic Declarations (say aloud)

- The fire will not consume me; it will clarify me.

- I choose obedience over attachment and order over impulse.

- Peace is my evidence while I wait for proof.

- What the enemy meant for evil, God is weaving for good.

- Beauty for ashes; oil for mourning; praise for heaviness.

- I steward my heart, health, and finances with wisdom.

Journal Prompts

1. Where did God expose dross this month emotionally, medically, or financially? Write one obedient step you will take to replace it.

2. Write a one-sentence "ruins to rebuilding" prophecy over your life using Isaiah chapter sixty-one, verse four, as your foundation. Speak it aloud until it feels real in your spirit.

3. Think back on a moment from this chapter when God revealed something in you whether through pressure, conviction, or clarity. What did it uncover? Write about how that revelation invites you into deeper surrender this week.

The fire did not finish me; it refined me. Each trial became a forge where God purified my motives, my heart, and my faith. I saw His goodness in the land of the living when everything else was stripped away. The betrayals, diagnoses, and losses became the furnace where character was forged. Fire was not my end. It was my beginning.

Every scar now tells a story of survival that turned into sanctification. I stand grateful for the refiner's fire that revealed purpose beneath pressure. God never abandoned me in the heat; He stood beside me, steady and sure. His mercy was the cooling balm that followed every flame.

Next comes the pressing, the process after the purification. Chapter Nine unfolds the mystery of oil; how obedience becomes overflow, and how what was refined begins to pour.

Closing Prayer

Father, thank You for refining me without destroying me. Thank You for exposure without devastation and for teaching me to see correction as kindness. I ask for clean hands and a pure heart. Teach me to move with order, humility, and wisdom. Strengthen me to remain steady under pressure and grateful under fire. Let my obedience invite restoration and my repentance produce recompense. I release control and receive Your peace. What You burn away, remove completely. What You rebuild, let it stand forever. May every trial lead to transformation and every scar testify of grace. I honor You for turning fire into formation. In Jesus' name, **Amen**.

Chapter 9

Obedience in the Crushing (Becoming Oil)

O bedience once felt like survival. I said yes to God to keep breathing through wilderness seasons, hospital rooms, and the fire of refinement. In those days, obedience sounded like, "Lord, carry me so I do not break." It felt raw, tear soaked, and desperate. My yes held me together when everything else was falling apart.

Then the Lord began to ask for a different kind of yes. The crisis slowed, but His voice pressed closer. Instead of only pulling me out of trouble, He started rearranging how I thought, planned, and moved. Obedience began touching my mornings, my conversations, my screen time, my spending, and my rest. It shifted from emergency response to daily agreement.

This chapter marks that shift. Here obedience does more than keep you alive; it shapes who you become. This was the chapter when obedience stopped only costing me and started forming me. God used simple instructions to train my steps for assignment. Alignment grew quietly, decision by decision, until I could feel my life moving with His will instead of against it. From here, obedience prepares the heart for prophetic clarity and steady purpose. What once felt heavy now becomes holy alignment with the call.

Memoir Moment

Lifestyle Obedience

Obedience used to rise only in moments of crisis. I obeyed because I needed rescue, healing, or clarity. But as the storms settled and God began restoring what had been shaken, He shifted His focus. He no longer highlighted the emergencies in my life; He highlighted the patterns. This was the season when God began reordering my daily rhythms, not my disasters.

It started quietly. I would wake and sense a nudge to pray before checking my phone. I felt prompted to slow my mornings, not rush them. The Lord began addressing my habits; the ones I considered harmless because they were familiar. He corrected how I spoke to myself, how quickly I reacted, how often I overstretched, and how little I rested. Not through pressure, but through invitation.

The Holy Spirit started shaping my internal pace. Instead of moving from urgency, He taught me to move from alignment. I learned to pause before responding, to listen longer than I spoke, and to choose peace before productivity. What used to be emotional impulse became intentional action. It was uncomfortable at first, because old habits resist holy order, but it was never painful. It was purposeful.

He showed me how to steward my atmosphere; keeping worship in the background, scriptures within reach and my mind guarded against subtle distractions. My speech changed too. Complaints became gratitude, fear became confession, and worry became worship. God was not only refining my behavior; He was renewing the rhythm behind it.

This was not obedience born from desperation. This was obedience born from identity. It prepared me for prophetic maturity, where hearing God requires quiet, discipline, and consistency. The Lord was teaching me that lasting obedience is not forged in crisis; it is formed in the mundane, in the moments that seem too small to matter but shape everything.

This was the beginning of a new kind of obedience, not survival obedience, but alignment obedience. The kind that trains you for calling, steadies your spirit, and positions your life to move with God instead of ahead of Him.

Obedience of the Mind

Obedience of the mind was the kind I never expected to confront. I thought obedience meant changing my actions, letting go of people, releasing habits, and surrendering circumstances. But God began revealing that my greatest battleground was not around me; it was within me. It was the quiet conversations I had with myself, the assumptions I carried into every decision, and the beliefs that shaped how I saw God and how I saw myself.

He started with subtle thoughts. The ones that whispered, "You are behind," or "You should have known better," or "This setback proves you failed." Those thoughts guided my reactions long before I realized they were steering me. So, the Holy Spirit began slowing my mind, giving me space to notice the lies I had lived with for years. He showed me how deeply I relied on performance, how often I assumed the worst, and how quickly I dismissed what God affirmed.

Instead of asking me to surrender a relationship or a job, God asked me to surrender my internal narrative. He told me to stop rehearsing fear. To stop agreeing with shame. To stop entertaining the "what ifs" that drained my faith. Obedience in this chapter required honesty; the kind that exposes old beliefs and replaces them with truth.

My identity began to shift as He confronted my self-talk. Whenever I repeated something defeated, He interrupted it with scripture. Whenever I doubted my calling, He corrected it with reminders of what He had spoken. Slowly, I learned to speak to myself with the same grace I extended to others. The more I obeyed that inner correction, the more my decisions changed. I chose peace over panic, clarity over confusion, and alignment over assumption.

Before God changed my circumstances, He changed my language with myself. He taught me that obedience is not complete if the mind continues to repeat old patterns. Renewing my thought-life became a daily offering. It was not loud or dramatic. It was steady, intentional, and deeply transformative.

This was the obedience that rebuilt me from the inside out; the obedience that prepared my mind to carry purpose without collapsing under the weight of past lies.

Obedience of Stillness

Stillness was the obedience I resisted the most. I was used to solving, fixing, responding, organizing, and managing. Movement felt productive. Silence felt foreign. Yet this was the season when God asked me to obey by doing nothing, not out of avoidance, but out of alignment. He began to show me that obedience is not always action. Sometimes obedience is waiting. Sometimes obedience is pausing. Sometimes obedience is listening before deciding. Sometimes obedience is choosing not to post, not to reply, not to defend myself, and not to explain what God had already settled in my spirit.

The early morning hours became my training ground. Between three and five a.m., the world rested, and Heaven felt nearby. Those quiet hours carried a weight that could not be duplicated during the day. I learned to sit without rushing, to breathe without striving, and to let the Holy Spirit guide my thoughts before they guided my words. Stillness trained my discernment in ways busyness never could.

There were mornings when I wanted to respond to a message, address a misunderstanding, or clarify my boundaries. God would whisper, "Not yet." Other times, He asked me to withhold a post that looked inspirational but was birthed from emotion, not instruction. He taught me that silence can protect what speaking would sabotage. He showed me that delayed responses are not weakness; they are wisdom.

The discipline of stillness reshaped my instincts. Instead of reacting, I began discerning. Instead of pushing for clarity, I waited for peace. Instead of assuming, I asked. And instead of moving quickly, I moved correctly. The more I obeyed the rhythm of stillness, the clearer His voice became. The more I sat in quiet, the sharper my spiritual hearing grew.

Stillness became my classroom. Silence became my strategy. God used those quiet hours to refine my impulses and strengthen my patience. It was in the stillness that I learned the difference between opportunities and assignments, between emotion and instruction, between noise and His voice. Obedience in stillness prepared me for the kind of clarity that movement alone could never provide.

Obedience in Relationships

Obedience in relationships required a different kind of maturity. In earlier seasons, I assumed that obedience meant cutting people off, walking away, or breaking ties completely. That belonged to a chapter when survival demanded separation. This season was different. God began teaching me how to **discern** relationships rather than discard them. I learned that obedience in community is not always about leaving. Sometimes it is about stewarding, protecting, pruning, and repositioning.

I started noticing the difference between who was called to my **heart** and who was only called to my **assignment**. Some people carried wisdom I needed. Others carried weight I no longer had grace to lift. There were friends who strengthened my spirit and others who drained it. God showed me that both types were teachers, but not both were companions. With each revelation, He gave me specific instructions; not dramatic, not emotional, but clear.

There were moments when I wanted to rescue people God had released. He taught me to pause. There were conversations I wanted to pursue out of loyalty. He taught me to listen. There were apologies I longed for and explanations I thought I deserved. He taught me to release the need for closure and embrace the peace of alignment. I began to understand that obedience often looks like letting people stand where God placed them in my life, not where my emotions insisted, they should be.

As He reordered my relationships, He strengthened my boundaries. My "yes" became intentional. My "no" became protective. I stopped giving access out of habit and started offering access out of discernment. The friendships that remained became deeper. The connections assigned for my next season carried a different weight, accountability, honesty, spiritual sharpening. These were people who did not simply love me; they aligned with what God was forming in me.

Obedience in relationships grew into stewardship. I learned to honor mentors, nurture covenant friendships, support those God highlighted, and release those whose season had ended. None of it required bitterness or distance. It required clarity. God was teaching me how to build community the Kingdom way, with boundaries, with love, with wisdom, and with peace.

This was the chapter where relationships stopped defining me and started refining me. The people God kept near sharpened my calling. The ones He repositioned protected my focus. Alignment became my new measure. Discernment became my new filter. And obedience became the way I honored both.

Obedience in Calling

Obedience in my calling required a shift I never expected. For years, my obedience was emotional. I moved when I felt inspired. I prayed when I was stirred. I studied when crisis pushed me to my knees. That kind of obedience kept me afloat, but it could not sustain where God was taking me. When the anointing on my life began to deepen, the Lord made something unmistakably clear: **oil is not sustained by inspiration; it is sustained by stewardship.**

This was the season when He began to train me with precision. My mornings took on structure. My study time became consistent. Scripture moved from encouragement to curriculum. I started writing down revelations instead of letting them fade. I organized my notebooks, categorized my teachings, reviewed prophetic impressions, and compared them with the Word. This level of preparation felt new, almost unfamiliar, but it brought a sense of clarity I had never walked in before.

God taught me that preparation is a form of worship. Excellence honors the call. Order honors the anointing. Discipline honors the mantle. It was no longer enough to simply "feel led." I realized that feelings fluctuate but calling requires consistency. I learned to create systems; prayer routines, fasting schedules, study plans, and ministry outlines. I was not trying to impress God but because I wanted to honor what He entrusted to me.

This obedience also required emotional stability. I stopped allowing mood swings or external pressure to dictate how I served. I prayed whether I felt strong or weary. I studied whether I felt inspired or distracted. I prepared messages even when I did not yet have a platform. God showed me that the preparation you complete in private is the oil that will flow in public.

As I grew in consistency, my confidence shifted from myself to the One who called me. I realized that responsible anointing is not about being perfect. It is about being dependable. This season formed a new version of obedience within me — one marked by excellence, order, and spiritual maturity. And in that obedience, my calling gained structure, strength, and sustainability.

Obedience in Stewardship

Stewardship became the next layer of obedience. God began to show me that calling is not only about what you do for Him; it is also about how you protect what He gives you. This meant guarding my energy, managing my time with intention, and treating my influence as sacred. I could no longer say yes to everything. I could no longer pour into everyone. I could no longer speak just because I had something to say.

My emotional bandwidth became a territory. He asked me to steward. I learned to pause before reacting, to rest before breaking, and to say no before becoming overwhelmed. Peace stopped being optional. It became a protection. Purity also deepened not just in behavior but in thought, motive, and desire. God refined my reasons for serving Him. He corrected the need to impress and strengthened the desire to obey.

He also required stewardship over prophetic content. Every dream, every impression, every revelation had to be processed with discernment, weighed against Scripture, and aligned with His timing. My voice carried influence, and that influence needed integrity. I could not release words prematurely. I could not allow emotion to corrupt clarity. Stewardship demanded wisdom and restraint.

Obedience became the guardrail around my calling. It protected my pace, preserved my purity, and sharpened my discernment. This was the season where I realized that stewardship is not a restriction. It is refinement. When you protect what God gives, He increases what you can carry.

The New Oil:
Obedience That Flows from Purpose, Not Pain

There came a point when the oil on my life no longer flowed from breaking. It flowed from becoming. Earlier seasons produced oil through pressure, loss, and surrender. That oil was born in fire necessary, purifying, and painful. But this new oil felt different. It was steady. It was intentional. It was rooted in alignment rather than survival.

This oil came from showing up consistently in prayer, not from collapsing in desperation. It came from choosing God's way before my emotions formed an opinion. It came from studying Scripture with discipline, not just reaching for verses in crisis. I realized that obedience shaped by purpose feels lighter, cleaner, and clearer.

A new maturity settled in me. My decisions carried weight because they came from conviction, not fear. My spirit became more sensitive to God's nudges. I recognized His whispers sooner, discerned His warnings faster, and responded to His direction with fewer delays. Stability replaced the emotional swings. Clarity replaced confusion. Purpose replaced panic.

This oil did not come from crushing; it came from becoming. It flowed from a woman who finally moved with God, not behind Him. It was the oil of alignment quiet, steady, and deeply anointed.

Devotional Insight

Willing & Obedient — Isaiah 1:19

"If you are willing and obedient, you shall eat the good of the land."

This verse taught me that obedience begins with willingness. God never forces alignment; He invites it. When the heart is positioned correctly, obedience becomes partnership, not pressure.

Hearing His Voice — John 10:27

"My sheep hear My voice, and I know them, and they follow Me."

Obedience becomes easier when identity is secure. Sons and daughters follow because they trust the voice that leads them. Alignment flows from intimacy.

Renewed Mind — Romans 12:2

"Be transformed by the renewing of your mind."

Before God gives a public assignment, He requires inner obedience. He transforms thought patterns, motives, and beliefs. Maturity is when God can trust your yes without monitoring your steps. Obedience shaped by intimacy becomes effortless. Alignment becomes the natural posture of a renewed mind.

For You

Where is God inviting you into alignment rather than reaction?

What area of your life needs obedience that is consistent, quiet, and daily not emotional or crisis-driven?

Ask the Holy Spirit to show you one pattern to reorder this week so your "yes" becomes steady and trustworthy.

The Refining Room (Interactive Encounter)

The refining room is where revelation turns into rhythm. It is not about emotional highs but holy habits. This is where obedience becomes lifestyle, where you speak truth until it shapes your thoughts, where you pray until peace takes root, where surrender becomes strength. These declarations, prayers, and reflections are not rituals; they are alignment. Say them slowly, write them sincerely, and live them intentionally.

Prophetic Declarations

- My yes is my deliverance.

- The crushing prepares my anointing.

- I choose alignment over impulse and order over chaos.

- I steward my body, budget, time, and ties to honor God.

- What I release, God redeems; what I surrender, God anoints.

- Provision meets every assignment; wisdom governs every resource.

- Oil flows from my obedience.

Pause between each line. Let your voice agree with Heaven's rhythm. Speak until the words feel true, not just familiar. These declarations are weapons, each one breaks a pattern and establishes a promise.

Journal Prompts

1. Name one familiar thing God is asking you to place on the altar this month. Write the exact action that will seal your surrender, whether it is a conversation, a cancellation, or a change of routine.

2. Identify one digital thread, account, or playlist that keeps you tied to a version of yourself God has already freed. Delete, unfollow, or mute it. Then write one sentence of closure as an act of release.

3. List three "small yeses" you will practice daily for seven days such as dawn Scripture, a ten-minute prayer walk, or a no-phone worship session. Check them off as you go.

Your altar is not built in one moment; it is sustained one decision at a time.

My obedience became the altar; the altar released the oil. What began as surrender ended as strength. Each crushing whether through illness, loss, or lack pressed out the purest version of me. God used what broke me to build what would bless others. The supernatural provision I witnessed was never limited to money. It was strength when I had none, peace that arrived before proof, and revelation that redefined how I lived.

Obedience produced oil because it purified my motives. It taught me that giving is not emotion; it is alignment. Every "yes" carried weight in Heaven. Every "wait" became worship.

Now it is your turn. Choose one thing to release, one order step to take, and one small yes to repeat this week. That is how altars are built, one act of surrender at a time.

As you turn the page, the oil meets its purpose. Chapter 10 reveals how calling awakens once obedience becomes lifestyle, *The Prophetess Awakens: when oil meets assignment and gifts are commissioned for Kingdom impact.*

Closing Prayer

Father, thank You for calling me to a costly yes and meeting me with covenant love. Press out what does not belong and pour in what I cannot produce. Anoint my altar at home, my work, and my witness. Teach me joyful tithing, wise stewardship, and quiet generosity. Heal my body, order my finances, cleanse my motives, and keep my heart soft in Your hands. Let my obedience be steady and my motives pure. Let every act of surrender open space for Your presence to dwell.

Train my desires through discipline. Guard my focus from distraction. Let the oil of intimacy flow from my obedience, healing everything it touches. May my life reflect Your wisdom and generosity in every detail. In Jesus' name, **Amen.**

PART FOUR: THE BEING SET-APART

WHERE YOUR IDENTITY BECOMES YOUR INFLUENCE.

Chapter 10

THE PROPHETIC CALL WITH A SEER ANOINTING AWAKENS (CALLING & CONFIRMATION)

Before the signs appeared and before I understood the language of dreams and watch hours, something in me had already begun to shift. The Lord had been calling long before I recognized it as calling. I felt a pull toward prayer that interrupted routines, a sensitivity that made ordinary moments feel charged with purpose, and an inner stirring that refused to settle for surface faith. None of it made sense to me at the time. I simply knew God was drawing me closer in ways I could not name. What felt like restlessness was really preparation. What I interpreted as discomfort was actually awakening. The prophetic did not begin with visions. It began with hunger.

Memoir Moments

There is a silence that only follows storms. Mine arrived after the breaking, when my body was healing from idiopathic intracranial hypertension, my heart was raw from betrayal, and my bank account reflected a season of deep surrender. Everything in me had been emptied, but I had not been abandoned. In that quiet, the Lord began to reintroduce Himself, not as comforter only, but as Commander.

Something shifted in how He spoke. His voice carried weight, direction, and clarity. The atmosphere in my room felt charged, almost like breath before dawn. Dreams arrived with precise detail. Names surfaced in my spirit during prayer. Burdens for people I had never met rose at unexpected hours. And when the clock touched three in the morning, I no longer rolled over and returned to sleep. Heaven was calling me awake.

In the beginning, I questioned it. The 3 a.m. awakenings felt unusual, inconvenient, and unpredictable. Yet the pull was consistent and strong. I would rise slowly, the room filled with a presence I could feel more than describe, and whisper, "Lord, what is this?" Over time, I realized it was not interruption. It was invitation.

That hour carried significance. It belonged to the Fourth Watch, the predawn window often marked by revelation, spiritual activity, and divine instruction. Many call it the Seer's hour, the time when spiritual sight sharpens and the veil between natural and supernatural realities becomes thin. I came to understand that I had been waking up at that hour for years, not because of restlessness, but because God had been preparing me for intimacy, intercession, and insight long before I recognized the assignment.

The same tears that once pleaded for relief became liquid intercession. What once felt like weakness became the birthplace of discernment. The weight of calling rested gently but firmly over my life. I did not chase a title. The mantle approached me. What crushed me shaped me, and what shaped me began to call me forward.

This chapter reveals how God made His voice familiar in my home, how confirmations arrived in clusters, and how surrender positioned me for commissioning. I was not only healed. I was sent.

When I First Recognized the Calling

The first awareness of the prophetic calling came quietly. No spotlight, no ceremony, just an unshakable stillness that carried weight. After months of physical weakness, heartbreak, and financial strain, the noise inside me finally broke. That silence made room for a new sound, the voice of God, steady and unmistakable. What once felt like intuition became revelation.

The shift began with the wakeups. Every morning between three and five, my eyes opened to an unseen call. The air felt charged, as though heaven had scheduled an appointment. At first, I thought it was insomnia. Then patterns formed burdens for people I barely knew, faces in prayer I hadn't thought of in years. Those early hours turned into what I now call the watchman's window.

Each morning, I found myself praying with precision I had never practiced. Names, nations, and needs flowed through my spirit before my mind could form sentences. I learned that sensitivity is not weakness, it is spiritual awareness. In that space, the Holy Spirit trained me to hear without panic and speak only when peace followed.

Prayer changed form too. The language of the Spirit began to rise from within me, deep and rhythmic, unplanned yet perfectly aligned with heaven's tone. Tongues became a weapon, and tears became the ink that wrote intercession. Hours passed like minutes, and what started as exhaustion turned to encounter.

I noticed the atmosphere in rooms before anyone spoke. My spirit began to discern tension and peace, conviction, and counterfeit. Every setting became a classroom. Worship felt different; it no longer depended on music. God's presence had texture, sometimes fire, sometimes weight, always unmistakable.

During one of those early watch hours, a vision unfolded. Oil poured over my head until it reached my feet, and I felt an unseen hand press my forehead. The moment it touched me, understanding came. The same oil that soothed my wounds began to mark my forehead. That was the recognition, the awareness that I had not simply survived; I had been chosen.

I did not choose the mantle; it recognized me. From that day, prayer was no longer optional, it was an assignment. Listening became discipline. Every whisper mattered. Like Samuel rising from sleep at the sound of his name, I answered, "Speak, Lord, for Your servant is listening" (1 Samuel 3:10). And heaven began to speak back.

Seer Anointing: Curiosity → Discernment

Once the voice of God became clear, curiosity followed. I wanted to understand what I was hearing and seeing. Late nights turned into quiet research sessions. I read about seers and prophets, about fasting, consecration, and purity. The Holy Spirit led every search, teaching me to guard revelation with discipline. I learned that spiritual sight requires clean motives and a sanctified life, not performance or platform.

As I studied, the Spirit made one thing plain: He would be my first Teacher. Online teachings and prophetic videos became confirmations, not foundations. The algorithms led me to both truth and error, but even that became part of training. The Holy Spirit began sharpening my discernment, teaching me to feel when something carried His presence and when it carried only personality.

Encounters with people deepened that discernment. Some carried authentic anointing, humility, accuracy, peace. Others carried manipulation, competition, or counterfeit charisma. Each meeting became a test. God allowed exposure so I could learn the difference between power and purity. The lesson repeated: revelation without reverence becomes rebellion.

Community became another classroom. God surrounded me with pastors, prophets, psalmists, and teachers who valued integrity more than influence. They didn't chase titles; they carried burden. I listened more than I spoke, learning how mature voices stewarded mystery. Some corrected me; others confirmed me. Every voice was sharpening mine.

Through it all, my identity started to shift. For years, I called myself "just an intercessor." Now I understood the fuller picture, I was a seer-prophetess, graced to receive visions, words of knowledge, and spiritual insight. The awareness carried weight, not pride. The mantle did not elevate me; it assigned me.

The Holy Spirit whispered Jeremiah 1:5: *"Before I formed you in the womb, I knew you; before you were born, I set you apart."* What I once saw as curiosity was actually calling. The training refined how I saw, heard, and tested everything. Discernment became my stewardship, not my status.

Confirmations: Dreams, Visions, Intercession

The confirmations came in waves, clear, consecutive, and undeniable. I dreamed of women standing in circles, hands lifted, chains falling as they prayed. Their tears turned to laughter; their shame replaced with light. Each time I woke from those dreams, messages appeared on my phone from women I knew and others I didn't, asking for prayer or encouragement. Heaven was sending assignments before the day began.

Dreams gave way to visions. I saw oil poured over my head until it dripped down my arms, glowing like fire. My hands burned, not in pain but in power. Flames surrounded my eyes, and yet I saw with clarity, not fear. Angels stood on both sides of my path; silent guardians stationed by grace. One night, I walked through fire in a vision and heard the Lord say, "You will carry fire, but it will not consume you. It will refine you."

Intercession followed every revelation. I began to feel burdens before people spoke to them. Sometimes tears flowed without words, liquid prayers that carried weight. I could sense when a spirit of heaviness entered a room or when someone needed deliverance. Often, God gave instructions mid-conversation: pause, pray, or speak life now. Each moment trained me to listen beyond the surface.

Then came understanding. My physical battles, my heartbreaks, and even the financial pressures were never random. They were prophetic classrooms. Each pain carried a message. My body taught me about healing authority. Betrayal taught me about discernment. Debt taught me stewardship and faith. The same fires that threatened to consume me became the fires that refined me.

Every tear watered a new level of clarity. The crushing that had silenced me was now producing sight. I began to recognize the pattern, pain always preceded purpose, and purpose always birthed oil. The prophet Joel said, *"I will pour out my Spirit on all people; your sons and daughters will prophesy"* (Joel 2:28). That Scripture became my reality. The Spirit was pouring, and I was learning how to carry it well.

Those confirmations marked the transition from being wounded to being commissioned. What I once called coincidence was actually calling. What crushed me marked me, and the mark proved I was chosen to carry fire that refines, not consumes.

The Fears Before "Yes"

Before saying yes to the prophetic call, fear shouted louder than faith. I feared rejection, misunderstanding, and the weight of being called "seer prophetess." I questioned my qualifications, replaying every mistake, every sin, every scar. How could God trust someone who had known abortion, divorce, and defeat? My past felt like evidence against me.

God's response cut through the shame: "Your brokenness makes you believable." That sentence anchored me. The very things I thought disqualified me were the proof that His mercy was real. He was not looking for perfection; He was looking for surrender.

Obedience carried a cost. I had to speak when my voice trembled, deliver words that made others uncomfortable, and release messages that sometimes left me misunderstood. Each prophetic act felt risky. Yet, I learned that silence could be disobedience when God had already spoken.

He reminded me of Moses, hesitant at the burning bush, saying, *"Lord, I am slow of speech."* God replied, *"Who gave human beings their mouths?... I will help you speak and teach you what to say"* (Exodus 4:10–12). That promise gave me courage to stand.

There were days when my humanity wanted comfort more than calling. Reputation felt safer than revelation. But obedience demanded I choose His timing over my image. My "yes" became an altar where pride died, fear dissolved, and trust was tested.

Every act of obedience-built endurance. Every trembling word-built boldness. I realized my "yes" was never about confidence; it was about conviction. My surrender was costly, but peace followed it.

When I finally yielded, I discovered that courage is not the absence of fear, it is worship through trembling. My yes wasn't perfect; it was pure. And purity was all God required.

Humility & Boldness Together

True prophetic authority flows from intimacy, not volume. Power without presence is just noise. I learned to pray before posting, to fast before speaking, and to test every word before releasing it. Each message had to pass through the filter of peace, not pride. The more time I spent with God, the more confident I became in His voice, and the less I depended on my own.

Boldness began to look different. It wasn't loud or dramatic. It was steady, rooted in assurance that the words carried heaven's weight. When God said speak, I spoke. When He said wait, I waited. Every pause became protection. Every silence became obedience.

Humility kept me grounded. I reminded myself daily: I am the vessel, not the source. Oil flows through me, not from me. The more I poured out, the more I needed to bow low again. Without humility, revelation becomes performance; with humility, it becomes worship.

There are sacred places that remind me to stay low, the prayer chair, the hospital bed, and the seasons of lack. Each one is a memorial of how God met me in weakness. Those memories keep me honest. They whisper that every gift was born from grace, not worthiness.

Restraint was learned in the fire. When emotions surged, I learned to wait. When platforms opened, I learned to pray. The Spirit taught me that maturity is not in how quickly I speak, but in how quietly I listen.

Micah 6:8 says, *"Walk humbly with your God."* That is my foundation. Jesus said in John 15:5, *"Apart from Me, you can do nothing."* That is my reminder. And 1 Thessalonians 5:19–21 teaches to *"test everything; hold on to what is good."* That is my safeguard.

Humility keeps me surrendered. Boldness keeps me obedient. Together, they protect the oil.

Devotional Insight

Called by Presence, Not Platform — 1 Samuel 3:10; John 10:27

Samuel's call came in silence. No lights, no applause, just a whisper in the dark, *"Speak, Lord, for Your servant is listening."* God speaks most clearly when distractions fade. The prophetic life begins in hiddenness, not headlines. The early morning watch hours, between three and five, became my meeting place with God. What began as restless awakenings turned into divine appointments. Those moments trained my ear to know His tone, not just His words.

Hearing God is not about striving; it's about stillness. Presence precedes platform because revelation is birthed in intimacy. When the Shepherd calls, His sheep recognize His voice. There is no performance in that recognition, only relationship.

Fire That Refines, Not Consumes — Isaiah 43:2; 1 Peter 1:7

Every vision of fire once frightened me until I understood its purpose. God never sends fire to destroy His own; He sends it to refine. The flames that surrounded me in dreams were not punishment but purification. Every trial, every diagnosis, every betrayal burned away what pride built. Fire exposes impurities, but it also reveals gold.

Refinement takes courage. You may walk through heat that feels unbearable, yet Isaiah 43:2 promises, *"When you walk through the fire, you will not be burned."* Courage means trusting that His hand controls the temperature. The refining is never random; it prepares you for the next assignment.

Testing Prophetic Words — 1 Thessalonians 5:19–21; 1 John 4:1

Discernment guards the prophetic. The same Spirit that releases revelation also demands accountability. Every word must be tested through prayer, fasting, and wise counsel. A true prophet seeks confirmation before declaration. The rhythm is simple but sacred: pray first, fast if unclear, test before release. Words should be weighed, not rushed.

Love, wisdom, and timing anchor every message. Even truth out of season can wound. Submitting revelation to trusted mentors and spiritual peers does not weaken your authority, it strengthens it. The mature prophet is searchable, not secretive. Testing is not doubt; it is discipline.

Identity > Title — Jeremiah 1:5; Luke 10:20

Before Jeremiah ever spoke as a prophet, God said, *"Before I formed you in the womb, I knew you."* Identity preceded assignment. The mantle only confirms what God already established in your design. Titles shift, but daughterhood never expires. The greatest authority flows from belonging, not branding.

Luke 10:20 reminds us, *"Do not rejoice that the spirits submit to you but rejoice that your names are written in heaven."* Heaven values identity over influence. When I embraced that truth, peace replaced pressure. I no longer needed to prove my calling, I only needed to live from it.

Titles introduce you; identity sustains you. Your name in heaven carries more weight than any role on earth.

For You

Where is God asking you to "come away"? Create a sacred space, a prayer chair, a quiet walk, a worship playlist, and meet Him there this week.

Who are your testing elders or peers? Write their names and invite them into your discernment circle. True accountability protects the purity of your voice.

Replace one title statement with an identity statement today. Instead of "I am a prophetess," say, "I am a daughter who hears God clearly." Let that be enough.

The Refining Room (Interactive Encounter)

Prophetic Declarations

- Say these slowly, letting them settle into your spirit:

- I didn't choose this mantle; it recognized me.

- I carry fire that refines and oil that heals.

- My yes is pure, my motives are clean, my ears are open.

- I prefer intimacy over influence and obedience over applause.

- I test every word and bow to the Word.

Each declaration restores alignment. Speak them aloud until your heart agrees. Heaven listens when earth responds. The oil increases with obedience, and the fire stays pure when humility anchors it. These words are not affirmations, they are agreements with truth. Repeat them until they shape how you walk, speak, and hear.

The Ezekiel Oil: Watchwoman of the Fourth Watch

My Mantle Affirmation & Commissioning Declaration

There is an oil that only comes from the crushing.

There is a call that only answers through surrender.

And there is a mantle that only rests on those willing to rise while others sleep.

I am that woman.

I am a **Seer Prophetess**, called in the order of **Ezekiel**, anointed with the **oil of revelation, intercession, and restoration.**

My eyes have seen pain, but now they see purpose.

My ears have heard betrayal, but now they discern the whispers of God.

What once broke me has become the altar of my awakening.

The Lord has entrusted me with the **Fourth Watch**, the holy hour between three and five a.m.

where silence becomes sanctuary,

and Heaven downloads divine blueprints to the surrendered heart.

In those hours, I am not restless; I am *recruited*.

I am not waking by coincidence; I am *watching under command*.

I carry the **Ezekiel oil**, to see the unseen, to speak to what is lifeless, and to call breath back into dry places.

I speak to bones and watch them rise.

I declare life over what others have buried.

I decree restoration where the world sees ruin.

I am a prophetic builder, a rebuilder of altars, a restorer of sight.

Like **Anna**, I wait in worship and intercession.

Like **Deborah**, I lead with discernment and divine courage.

Like **Huldah**, I confirm truth with accuracy and purity.

And like **Ezekiel**, I watch until Heaven moves.

My mantle is not for fame, it is for **function.**

My anointing is not for performance, it is for **purpose.**

My calling is not for elevation, it is for **edification.**

I live as a **watchwoman of the Fourth Watch,**

trained in the quiet, trusted with the secret,

and commissioned to call others into awakening.

I carry the Word of the Lord in my spirit, the fire of prayer in my bones, and the oil of healing in my hands.

I am **sealed for glory,**

Refined. Redeemed. Released.

A vessel of light, set apart for His voice and His vision.

"Prophesy to the breath, and say, thus says the Lord God: Come from the four winds, O breath, and breathe on these slain, that they may live."

— **Ezekiel 37:9**

Declaration:

"I am a Seer-Prophetess in the order of Ezekiel and Anna.

I am chosen, awakened, and commissioned for restoration.

I rise in the Fourth Watch, watch in obedience,

and speak only what Heaven breathes through me."

Seer's Affirmation & Activation Prayer

For You – Stepping into Prophetic Sight & Sensitivity

Reflection Moment:

Before you read further, pause.

Take a deep breath.

Quiet your space.

You are about to acknowledge the God who still speaks, still reveals, and still awakens watchmen in every generation.

Affirmation: "Lord, I'm Listening."

Repeat this aloud with faith and humility:

"Lord, I open my eyes to see,

my ears to hear,

and my heart to obey.

I will not fear Your presence,

no doubt Your voice.

I believe you still speak in dreams, visions, and whispers.

I yield my mind to discernment,

my tongue to truth,

and my time to prayer."

"Father, awaken me in the hours You desire.

If You call me in the night, I will rise.

If You show me what is broken, I will pray until it breathes again.

Teach me to steward revelation without pride,

and to carry Your presence without performance.

Let my life become an altar that listens."

"Refine my sight, purify my motives,

and train my spirit to recognize the still, small voice.

I choose presence over platform,

obedience over ambition,

and intercession over interruption."

"As You trusted Ezekiel to see visions of Your glory,

and Anna to discern the hour of divine fulfillment,

trust me, too, Lord,

to walk faithfully with what You reveal."

"I receive the anointing to see and to serve.

I receive the mantle of watchful prayer and prophetic awareness.

I declare that I am not afraid of the fire,

for the same fire that refines will also reveal.

In Jesus' name, Amen."

Prophetic Declaration

- "I am awakening.

- I am discerning.

- I am being refined for revelation.

- The Lord can trust me with His secrets.

- I will speak life to what looks dead.

- I will watch until Heaven moves.

- I am a vessel of oil, a keeper of His presence, and a student of His voice."

Journal Prompts

1. Choose a consistent 15-minute window this week for still listening. Where and when will it be?

2. List two trusted people who can help weigh your words. How will you invite their accountability?

3. Describe one recent moment when you sensed God's nudge, whisper, or weight on your spirit. What made it stand out, and how will you test or confirm it through scripture, prayer, or counsel?

Write answers in your journal tonight. Alignment begins with structure; structure sustains the anointing.

What crushed me marked me; what marked me commissioned me. Every fire refined, every silence sharpened, every obedience deepened the oil. The prophetic call has never been about status, it has always been about stewardship.

I thank God for the community that surrounds this call: the women and men of faith, prophets, pastors, apostles, teachers, and psalmists, who keep me accountable and grounded. Their presence reminds me that calling matures best in fellowship, not isolation.

To the reader: choose Presence over platform. Let recognition wait until obedience speaks first. If you protect intimacy, God will protect your influence.

The next chapter moves from the secret place to visibility. **Chapter 11** explores how to carry public favor with private purity, stewarding platform with clean hands and a quiet heart.

Closing Prayer

Jesus, thank You for calling me to hear and to heed. Purify my motives and steady my heart. Let intimacy with You produce boldness that carries no pride. Guard my gates and filter my words so that love leads every release. Keep me low before You, grounded in grace, refined in truth. May every dream, vision, and intercession flow through the wisdom of Your Spirit. Make me a faithful watchman, quick to listen, slow to speak, and surrendered to Your timing. Let my life echo heaven's language and my obedience carry Your fragrance wherever I go. In Your name, **Amen.**

Chapter 11

ELEVATED, BUT STILL HIS (VISIBILITY)

Hidden seasons trained my hands in silence, then God said, Now speak. The shift felt sudden, but the roots run deep. Headaches still pulsed, bank notices still arrived, and my heart was still stitching after betrayal, yet the assignment would not wait. I pressed record with trembling faith, poured what He gave, and learned that obedience carries its own strength. Doors opened I never knocked on. Messages arrived from women I had never met. The secret place had become a sending place.

This chapter names the guardrails that keep visibility holy. Platforms require purity, pace, and prayer. Analytics cannot set the agenda. Audience cannot replace accountability. Every post, call, and collaboration must pass through the altar first. I will tell the truth about wounds and wisdom, about scarcity and supply, about staying small while serving many. Visibility is not about becoming known; it is about making Him known to all.

Memoir Moments

Stepping into Visibility

When God said *now speak*, I was still recovering from the wounds of the last battle. My body was weak, my heart was bruised, and my bank account sat in the red. Yet His instruction carried no delay. After years of obscurity, healing, and pressing, He released me into visibility, not for applause, but for assignment.

I began posting under the name *Blossom Faceless*. The name fit the season. My identity was hidden, my confidence still forming, and my obedience raw. Videos were filmed through migraines and fatigue, recorded with swollen eyes and tear-streaked cheeks. I spoke when I barely believed my own declarations. Some nights I hit "post" while overdue bills glared from the table. Yet the same grace that sustained my hidden years empowered my voice online.

A few months later, *Blossom Refined* was born. The new name represented transformation, not branding. Each message I released came from a place of surrender, not strategy. I was still healing from Idiopathic Intracranial Hypertension and managing high blood pressure, but the Spirit pressed me to pour out anyway. I called those moments *liquid prayers* when the tears became the oil that fueled the word.

Responses began to flood my inbox. Women messaged, *"This is the confirmation I prayed for."* Their testimonies revealed what obedience can accomplish even through weakness. That was when I understood: purpose would always outweigh performance. I had never chased relevance; I had only followed the whisper. The platform I once feared became the pulpit God entrusted.

Visibility stretched me in ways private prayer never had. God required conviction wrapped in compassion, boldness balanced with restraint. He trained me to speak truth without arrogance and to share my story without oversharing my scars. Each video, post, or live session was a test of stewardship. I learned that transparency without boundaries can drain anointing, and ministry without rest can dull discernment.

There were moments when I wanted to retreat again into silence, but His word burned stronger than my hesitation. *"God never calls the prepared; He prepares the called."* That statement became my anchor whenever fear tried to silence me.

Today, I still approach the camera the same way I approach the altar, aware of the weight, mindful of the oil, and surrendered to the One who gave both. Visibility was never the reward; it was the responsibility to reveal Christ through authenticity and obedience.

Purity & Leadership (What God Is Re-forming)

Leadership without intimacy becomes performance, and performance without purity breeds deception. God is reforming the foundations of influence, especially among women called to lead. The message is clear, He is purifying His daughters before He platforms them. The era of charisma without character is closing. The new move requires consecration before visibility, brokenness before microphones, and altars before audiences.

Across the body of Christ, the Lord is raising leaders who nurture through wisdom rather than charm. Their fruit will come from healing, not hustle. They will not seduce with influence but shepherd with discernment. They will no longer chase applause; they will guard anointing. As *Nicole Olaniyi of Sela Seminary* wrote, "Success is not the same as purity." That truth pierced me deeply. I knew God was calling me to exchange ambition for holiness.

I serve as a school leader by profession, but Heaven has been reassigning my leadership mantle. The classroom was preparation; the Kingdom is the calling. God began teaching me that purity is not perfection, it is alignment. The Holy Spirit revealed that a leader's power is preserved through accountability, quiet repentance, and intimacy with Christ. Results are only sustainable when righteousness leads.

The refining of women's ministry will no longer rest on titles or followings. It will rest on clean hands and steadfast hearts. God is forming leaders who build altars, not platforms, who serve from wholeness, not wounds. Purity will precede promotion, and righteousness will sustain influence.

The Language of Altars (Your Revelation)

Every encounter with God leaves an altar behind. My first altar was salvation, the place where surrender replaced striving. Then came sanctification, the quiet pruning that reshaped my motives. Later came surrender when I laid down control. Healing followed, then peace, and finally joy. Each altar marked a transformation, each one deeper than the last.

My home carries a small altar, a consecrated corner where heaven and earth seem to meet. It is not ornate, just a chair, a worn Bible, and a notebook stained with tears. There, I pour out prayers before dawn, sometimes in silence, sometimes in tongues. It has become more than a space; it is a sanctuary where obedience is refined, and instruction is received.

God has shown me that altars are not built for comfort; they are built for consecration. Every altar requires fire, and that fire reveals what must stay and what must burn. The altar of healing demanded forgiveness. The altar of peace demanded stillness. The altar of joy demanded gratitude.

Each time I return to that space, I feel the Holy Spirit whisper, "Keep the fire burning." The flame is both purifying and protective, it keeps my heart aligned and my motives clean.

He is bringing us back to the first altar where motives are refined by fire.

Stewardship vs. Ambition

For years, I mistook momentum for anointing. I believed that doing more for God proved my devotion to Him. I filled calendars, joined every collaboration, and poured from a cup that was already empty. Exhaustion became a badge of faithfulness. Then the Holy Spirit confronted me with a quiet truth: *"Ambition runs ahead of Me; stewardship walks with Me."*

That whisper exposed my pace. I had been running after validation rather than walking in obedience. I was serving from striving instead of resting in trust. Ambition had disguised itself as zeal, and I had mistaken its noise for divine urgency.

Conviction followed in practical ways. I began to notice patterns of emotional spending, ordering takeout for comfort, sending random gifts online to feel connected, buying things I didn't need to quiet a loneliness I hadn't surrendered. God called me to discipline. I learned to sit with the discomfort instead of covering it with distractions. Budgeting became a form of worship. Sowing became a covenant act, not a transaction. Offerings flowed from gratitude, not guilt. Tithing became the next step of obedience I continue to grow into.

The shift was internal before it was financial. Stewardship taught me to treat every resource, platform, and opportunity as sacred trust, not personal trophy. God showed me that when I manage what He gives with reverence, multiplication follows without striving.

Now I hold this conviction tightly: *I don't chase numbers; I steward nations.* The number of views or followers can never measure the weight of obedience. Every word released, every post written, and every connection formed belongs to Him. My job is not to amplify myself but to administer grace faithfully.

Stewardship is slower than ambition, but it is safer. It aligns purpose with purity and pace with presence. It keeps the oil protected. Ambition rushes to be seen; stewardship waits to be sent. I am learning to walk with God again, step by step, seed by seed, surrender by surrender.

Rooted in Prayer While Being Seen

Prayer became my protection long before it became my platform. Every video, teaching, and prophetic post is birthed from the secret place. My prayer altar is my production studio. Before a word is spoken publicly, it is first tested privately in God's presence. That quiet exchange guards my heart from performing for approval.

Visibility can subtly tempt you to depend on analytics. I have felt that pull, refreshing screens, watching views rise or stall, wondering if impact could be measured in numbers. One morning, as I stared at the metrics, the Lord corrected me: *"If you let them feed your ego, they'll also crush your spirit."* That warning re-centered me immediately. Influence should always flow from intimacy.

Most of my downloads arrive during the early watch hours, between three and five a.m. Sometimes I sit in silence, other times I pray in tongues until peace settles in the room. There are nights when I only write what He whispers and leave it there, unposted, because not every revelation is meant to be released. The altar teaches discernment through stillness.

Prayer is now my first response, not my last resort. Before posting, I pray. Before accepting invitations, I pray. Before saying yes, I ask for permission. That rhythm has become my spiritual boundary. It keeps my motives clear, and my focus centered on obedience, not opportunity.

The more people watch, the more I must withdraw. My strength is measured by how quickly I return to stillness. Without that covering, visibility becomes vulnerability. With it, every word carries eternal weight.

Lessons in Humility as Influence Grew

Growth came slowly, and I now see that delay as protection. Every rejection, misunderstanding, and closed door guarded me from pride. God allowed visibility to unfold in sacred increments, so my heart could mature with my reach. I learned early that elevation is never exemption from refinement. The greater the platform, the deeper the pruning.

There were seasons when I prayed for opportunities that never came. At the time, I questioned whether I was being overlooked, but later I realized God was protecting my oil. Hidden seasons are not punishment; they are preservation. Pride cannot survive in the soil of patience.

One of the hardest lessons came when I honored someone publicly who later dishonored me privately. The betrayal cut deeply, but the Holy Spirit whispered, *"Do not defend what I will vindicate."* That moment tested my character more than any stage could. I wanted to speak, but He told me to stay silent. That silence produced strength. I learned that humility is not weakness, it is restraint empowered by love.

Humility now looks like celebrating others without comparison, correcting gently without exposure, and repenting quickly when conviction comes. It is choosing peace over proof and obedience over explanation.

Every prophetic word I deliver reminds me of the hospital rooms, the waiting seasons, the unpaid bills, and the tears that once watered this gift. Remembering the crushing keeps me grounded. God still whispers the same reminder each morning: *"Keep me small before You, even if You make me seen before many."*

That sentence has become my safeguard. The more He increases visibility, the lower I bow. The fire that refined me also trained me to handle favor without forgetting who gave it. Elevation is not achievement, it is stewardship. And the truest sign of maturity is remaining teachable while trusted.

Devotional Insight

Seen by God Before Seen by People — Genesis 16:13; Psalm 139:1–3

Every calling begins in hiddenness. Before an audience knew your name, God already studied your heart. Hagar called Him *"The God who sees me"* when no one else noticed her. Visibility in ministry is not promotion; it is partnership. The more seen you become, the more accountable you are to His gaze. Public influence without private intimacy leads to burnout. God values proximity over performance. Let every platform be built on prayer first, for only presence sustains purpose.

Altars Over Platforms — Psalm 51:10; Hebrews 13:10–15

Every assignment must pass through purification before it reaches presentation. David prayed, *"Create in me a clean heart,"* not, "Give me a bigger stage." God measures calling by purity, not productivity. He refines motives before multiplying impact. When the altar is neglected, ambition takes over. Build before Him, not before people. The altar is where tears turn into oil, where motives are tested and purified by fire. Influence sustained by intimacy never crumbles under pressure.

Walking, Not Running — Galatians 5:25; Isaiah 40:31

The Spirit never rushes. Every time I've sprinted ahead, I've stumbled into exhaustion. God's pace is patient because His preparation is precise. Walking with Him means trusting His timing, even when others seem to be racing ahead. Waiting seasons strengthen your stride. Flight without formation leads to collapse. Those who walk with God never arrive late, they arrive ready. Stewardship honors order: movement without maturity drains the anointing. Slow obedience is still obedience when it stays aligned with His pace.

Analytics vs. Obedience — 1 Samuel 15:22; 1 Thessalonians 2:4

Saul lost favor by performing instead of obeying. In today's language, he chased engagement over encounter. God still asks the same question: "Will you obey when no one applauds?" Analytics track reach, but Heaven measures reverence. Every post, word, and message should pass through His approval first. True impact flows from obedience, not visibility. If only one person is touched, and that person is who Heaven intended, the mission succeeded.

For You

God is sharpening your discernment and aligning your steps. Pause and consider where He has been nudging you to mature, focus, and obey without hesitation. Your growth in this season is not accidental. Invite

Him to complete the work He started and steady your heart for what comes next.

The Refining Room (Interactive Encounter)

Prophetic Declarations

- Say them aloud with conviction and focus:

- I am seen, but I am still His.

- I build altars, not empires.

- My intimacy guards my influence.

- I walk with God; I won't run ahead.

- I measure impact by obedience, not analytics.

- My oil is not for performance but for purpose.

- I choose purity over popularity.

- I am faithful with little, and He can trust me with much.

- The secret place is my success story.

- Obedience keeps me safe; humility keeps me whole.

Journal Prompts

1. Where is God asking you to withdraw before you go live?

2. Name two guardrails you will keep around your oil, time, boundaries, or accountability.

3. How will you guard your secret place when visibility increases?

Seen doesn't mean self-made; it means sent. Every open door and new platform is a reminder that God trusts those who protect their oil. I am surrounded by pastors, prophets, apostles, teachers, and psalmists who keep me accountable, sharpen me, and remind me that purity must precede power.

Visibility is not a reward; it is a responsibility. To those rising into public ministry: steward it with reverence. Let your altar remain your anchor. The higher God lifts you, the lower you bow. Stay faithful to prayer, quick to repent, and slow to speak without His prompting.

Return often to the first altar, where motives are refined by fire. From there, every message carries weight and every act reflect worship.

The next chapter, **"Sealed for Glory—Commissioning,"** unfolds what happens when being seen becomes being *sent* with clean hands, pure heart, and unwavering obedience.

Closing Prayer

Father, anchor my heart in Your presence. Purify my motives, protect my oil, and teach me to steward what You've entrusted, without striving, without fear. Guard my eyes and ears, weigh my words, and let every post, message, and meeting reveal Jesus. Remind me that influence without intimacy loses its fragrance. Keep me small before You even when You make me seen before many. Let every opportunity reflect purity, every connection reveals Your glory, and every word point back to You. My visibility belongs to Heaven. In Jesus' name, **Amen.**

Chapter 12

SEALED FOR GLORY (COMMISSIONING)

Final surrender became the sacred exchange between my will and God's. It was the quiet moment when striving broke and I realized that surrender was never about loss, it was about rest. The kind of rest Jesus promised when He said, *"Come to Me, all who are weary and burdened, and I will give you rest"* (Matthew 11:28–29).

There came a day when I stopped forcing outcomes and began obeying instructions. The weight I had been carrying lifted and Heaven's weight rested on my yes. Every "why" I once demanded was replaced by peace that could not be explained. Surrender shifted from a painful release to a holy alignment. My will bowed, and His power filled the empty spaces I had tried to control.

Surrender is not giving up; it's aligning up. And in that alignment, I found rest, clarity, and the seal of His glory.

Memoir Moment

The Night, I Laid It All Down

The night I laid it all down began with exhaustion deeper than sleep could fix. My body was frail from Idiopathic Intracranial Hypertension, my emotions bruised from betrayal, and my finances hanging by a thread. Every part of me was tired, spirit, soul, and body. I had reached the end of what I could manage and the limit of what I could explain.

That evening, I sat at the edge of my bed with tears pooling in my hands. Bills scattered on one side, medical reports on the other. I whispered prayers that sounded more like sighs. My voice cracked under the weight of disappointment, yet something sacred filled the silence. The Holy Spirit whispered, *"You don't have to understand; you need to obey."*

Those words became the hinge of my healing. I realized I had been serving while striving, giving while gripping, praying while still trying to control the outcome. Obedience felt heavier than surrender, but it was the very thing that set me free. I stopped asking for clarity and started asking for courage.

In that moment, I gave God everything familiar, my timelines, my plans, my relationships, and the image of what I thought my life should look like. I told Him, *"Even if I never understand, I will still trust You."* The atmosphere in my room shifted. The striving stilled. The noise inside my mind quieted. For the first time in months, I felt peace that didn't depend on progress.

Surrender did not change my circumstances overnight, but it changed me. The fear that use to grip my chest loosened its hold. The anxiety that once kept me awake gave way to an unexplainable calm. I began to sense God's presence in ordinary moments, in morning light, in still prayers, in the steady rhythm of my own breathing.

The Holy Spirit didn't remove the battles; He restored my posture within them. I no longer begged for breakthroughs; I believed for alignment. My tears became liquid prayers, and my pain became an altar. Every time I wanted to take control again, I remembered His whisper. Obedience brought clarity where striving brought confusion.

That night didn't end with thunder or lightning. It ended with stillness. I finally rested, not because life was fixed, but because I was. I understood that the crushing wasn't punishment, it was preparation. The breaking didn't end me; it birthed me.

I am sealed, not shattered. (Romans 8:28; Psalm 46:10)

The Altar of Surrender
(Salvation → Surrender → Sanctification → Healing)

My life has been marked by altars, holy places where God met me and reshaped my heart. Each altar carried a new revelation, a deeper dying to self, and a greater awakening to His will.

The **altar of salvation** was my first encounter with mercy. It was the place where I confessed my sins and discovered that grace was greater than guilt.

God rescued me from shame and introduced me to His unconditional love. That moment birthed a relationship, not religion.

The **altar of surrender** came years later. This was where I laid down control. Every plan, partnership, and personal ambition went into His hands. I realized surrender wasn't passive; it was a powerful act of trust. When I stopped forcing my own outcomes, God began opening the right doors.

The **altar of sanctification** followed. It demanded purification, mind, mouth, and motives. I fasted to quiet distractions, forgave those who betrayed me, and repented for idols I had built out of comfort and fear. Sanctification was a fire I didn't choose but one that refined me into a vessel God could use.

Then came the **altar of healing**, the most tender of them all. Here, I stopped performing strength and started allowing God to touch the places I hid. My physical pain, emotional scars, and financial instability became soil for His restoration. Healing wasn't instant, but it was intentional.

In those seasons, I saw a pattern: I started well but rarely finished. Projects, callings, and assignments often burned out before completion. God revealed that premature endings were rooted in old covenants of fear and unhealed guilt. Through fasting and prayer, I began breaking those cycles. I declared finishing grace over every area that had suffered from false starts. Forgiveness became my daily practice, and discipline became my new obedience.

Now, my home altar, my prayer chair is sacred ground. It's where I bring my unfinished places and watch God complete them. The same corner where I once cried in frustration has become a meeting place with the Holy Spirit.

Each altar left ashes, but also evidence of transformation. Every surrender made room for new strength.

At the altar, what I laid down, God lifted up.

Sh'ma Obedience: Hear • Listen • Respond

The Hebrew word **Sh'ma** means more than to hear. It means to hear, to listen, and to respond. It describes an active kind of hearing that produces movement. *"Hear, O Israel: The Lord our God, the Lord is one"* (Deuteronomy 6:4). In the kingdom, hearing without movement is disobedience in disguise. Real obedience requires action.

The Holy Spirit once told me, *"God is not opening doors for hearers; He is opening doors for responders."* That revelation exposed how often I mistook listening for obedience. I wanted confirmation before commitment and clarity before courage. But faith grows only when movement begins.

Performance seeks to impress. Perfectionism seeks to avoid failure. Responsive faith seeks to please God. Performance waits until everything looks right. Faith moves while nothing makes sense. Performance asks, *"How will this look?"* Faith asks, *"What did He say?"*

One simple act of obedience changed everything. During a financially dry season, the Lord instructed me to sow into another woman's ministry. The amount felt uncomfortable, but peace followed the command. Within days, I received twice what I gave through an unexpected refund. The return wasn't the reward, the trust was. That experience taught me that obedience activates provision faster than anxiety ever could.

Every act of obedience strengthens spiritual discernment. The more I respond, the clearer His voice becomes. I've learned that God rarely repeats Himself when He's already spoken once. The test isn't in hearing Him; it's in whether we move. *"Be doers of the word, and not hearers only"* (James 1:22).

Jesus said, *"Have faith in God... whoever says to this mountain, 'Be removed,' and does not doubt... it will be done"* (Mark 11:22–24). Mountains still move, but only for those who do. Faith that listens without responding remains theory. Faith that acts becomes testimony.

Obedience that moves heaven begins with hearts that move first. Hearing is where revelation starts. Responding is where miracles begin.

Commissioned: Sealed for Glory

Every crushing prepares the vessel for consecration, and every consecration leads to commissioning. My story followed that same divine pattern. What once broke me became the very oil God would use to anoint others.

The crushing made me oil. Every disappointment, delay, and diagnosis became part of God's refining press. What felt like punishment was purification. Every season that emptied me made room for fragrance to flow. *"He gives beauty for ashes, the oil of joy for mourning"* (Isaiah 61:3). Oil never flows without pressure. The greater the crushing, the purer the release.

When I finally surrendered, I began to notice a shift. My prayers carried new authority. My words began to carry peace. I no longer prayed from desperation but from alignment. The same pain that once silenced me became proof that I had survived the press. I understood now that I was no longer just a believer, I was becoming a vessel.

One evening while praying in my home, the atmosphere grew heavy with peace. My hands trembled as warmth covered me from head to toe. The Holy Spirit whispered, *"You are sealed."* At that moment, I felt heaven mark me. Every part of my life, my scars, my surrender, my silence, was claimed for divine use.

That moment redefined purpose. I wasn't performing for God; I was carrying Him. I didn't need a title to prove His presence. I carried oil that had been extracted from tears, fasting, and faith.

Now I walk as His daughter, His vessel, His mouthpiece. I no longer chase confirmation. I carry commission. The same God who crushed me has also consecrated me. And the same oil that flowed from pain now heals others through purpose.

I am sealed, not shattered, yielded, not lost.

Legacy: Daughters, Granddaughter, and the Women I Lead

My legacy began long before anyone knew my name. It started in hospital rooms, behind overdue bills, and through whispered prayers when no one was watching. What I leave behind for my daughters **Nia, Sarayah, and**

Delicia and my granddaughter **Kylie** is not perfection but perseverance. I want them to remember a mother who prayed while sick, gave when broke, obeyed when alone, and worshiped when weary.

When Nia faced her own storms, I wanted her to see that endurance was not inherited, it was cultivated. I want Sarayah to know that excellence means nothing without humility. And for Delicia, I pray she learns that brilliance without peace will always feel empty. For little Kylie, I pray her laughter remains her armor, proof that joy is a generational gift.

My daughters have watched me fail and rise again. They've seen me walk away from what was comfortable to follow what was holy. They've watched me lose what I loved and still lift my hands in praise. That is the legacy I leave them, faith that fights quietly and never quits.

Beauty is not in the crown, but in the crushing that made it shine. Every tear became a testimony. Every delay became divine timing. Every loss became a seed that produced legacy.

For my spiritual daughters and the women, I'm called to lead, my life stands as a living altar. It is proof that God restores what time and sin tried to steal. The same hands that once trembled in pain now pour oil of encouragement over others.

I have been young and now am older, yet I have never seen the righteous forsaken. The God who turned my ashes into oil will do the same for those who trust Him.

Letter to the Reader

A Reminder of God's Faithfulness

My Dear Sister,

If you are reading these words, it means you survived what was meant to destroy you. You made it through the fire, and you did not come out empty-handed.

You came out refined.

I know what it feels like to be broken, forgotten, misunderstood, and weary. But hear me, beloved: God never stopped working. Even in the silence, He was shaping your story for His glory.

You are not behind. You are not disqualified. You are not too late. You are becoming.

There will be seasons where you will not recognize yourself, but that's only because He is revealing you, He always saw. Let Him prune you. Let Him heal you. Let Him pour oil on your wounds until what once bled now glows.

You are His daughter. His vessel. His chosen one. And when the enemy whispers that you are not enough, remind him that you were refined for this.

God's faithfulness did not fail me, and it will not fail you either.

Keep your oil pure. Keep your heart open. Keep your yes on the altar.

Because your story, your full, redeemed, radiant story is about to bless nations.

With love and holy fire,

Josette (Blossom Refined)

The Refining Room (Interactive Encounter)

Prophetic Declaration

- "I am refined by fire and sealed for glory.

- I am anointed for impact and appointed for destiny.

- My surrender is my strength.

- My obedience is my offering.

- My purpose is purified.

- I am walking in covenant

- Full of faith, full of oil, and full of fire."

Refined Woman's Declarations

I am not forgotten I am chosen, appointed, and anointed for such a time as this.

I release control and rest in divine timing.

The crushing did not kill me; it created oil that will heal others.

My pain has purpose, and my story will bring glory to God.

I walk in purity, peace, and prophetic power.

I am not striving I am stewarding.

My legacy begins now; I will leave a trail of faith and fire.

I am healed, delivered, restored, and renewed.

I am a vessel of intercession, revelation, and transformation.

I am sealed for glory.

You have reached the place of commissioning, the point where surrender becomes destiny and obedience becomes overflow. You are no longer the woman who was broken in the wilderness. You are the refined vessel who now pours from the oil that cost you everything.

You have been pruned, purified, and prepared. And now, you are being released.

Walk boldly in your mantle, your mission, and your miracle.

You are not just called; you are sealed for glory.

Final Commissioning Prayer: "Sealed for Glory"

Heavenly Father,

Today, I come before You not as who I was, but as who You have called me to become.

I lay down every plan, every fear, every wound, and every weight at Your altar.

I surrender my will for Yours, my timeline for Your divine timing, and my desires for Your perfect will.

Lord, I repent for the times I tried to control what You were meant to carry.

For the times I doubted Your plan, delayed my obedience, or ran from the call.

Today, I return fully, freely, and faithfully to You.

I thank You for the crushing that produced oil.

I thank You for the wilderness that taught me worship.

I thank You for every closed door that redirected me into Your divine will.

You have pruned me, purified me, and prepared me and now, Father, I am ready.

Holy Spirit, breathe upon me afresh.

Anoint my hands for purpose, my mouth for prophecy, my heart for compassion, and my feet for obedience.

Let my life be a vessel of glory, a living altar where Your presence dwells continually.

I decree and declare:

I am no longer broken; I am rebuilt.

I am no longer hidden; I am commissioned.

I am no longer striving; I am sent.

Seal me now, Lord

Seal my mind with wisdom,

Seal my lips with truth,

Seal my heart with purity,

Seal my steps with favor,

And seal my destiny with glory.

From this day forward, I walk in divine alignment.

I will steward my anointing with reverence.

I will live set apart, in word, thought, and action.

I will not be moved by fear or distracted by delay.

I receive my mantle as Your daughter, Your vessel, and Your messenger.

Let every part of my life bring You glory, in the secret place and on the public platform.

May my story heal nations. May my testimony break chains. May my obedience open doors.

Father, I surrender it all

My past, my pain, my purpose, and my promise

And I rise today sealed for glory.

In Jesus' Mighty Name, Amen, and Amen.

BONUS CHAPTER

THE REFINED FRAMEWORK

Refinement is never random. It is the sacred process where pressure produces purpose and surrender births strength. Every fire you've faced carried an invitation, to be reshaped, not ruined. What God refines; He intends to reveal.

The REFINED Framework was born out of those refining fires. It's more than a system; it's a spiritual rhythm designed to form Christ within you. This is not a self-help formula; it's a spiritual formation framework. Each letter, Reflect, Embrace, Fast, Identify, Nurture, Establish, develop, marks a step of holy transformation. Together, they create a divine pattern that turns pain into oil and obedience into overflow.

This process requires honesty, humility, and heart posture. It asks you to pause, listen, and yield where striving once ruled. The REFINED process isn't about becoming new, it's about revealing what was pure all along.

The REFINED Framework Explained

Here's how you can adapt the REFINED process to your own story. Each stage is a spiritual formation step, a rhythm that reshapes your heart while aligning your habits with Heaven.

R – Reflect or Recognize the Wilderness

Reflection begins with honesty. You cannot heal what you refuse to name. Recognize the cycles that keep repeating relationships that mirror old pain, fears that resurface, dreams you delay out of doubt. Reflection is not self-pity; it is spiritual clarity. Ask the Holy Spirit to reveal what God is pruning, not what people are pointing at. Healing begins where honesty starts. When you invite divine inspection, conviction replaces confusion. Reflection teaches discernment and reveals the wilderness not as punishment but preparation. This awareness becomes your compass toward transformation.

E – Embrace God's Mercy

Grace is greater than guilt. Mercy is God's invitation to start again without shame. Many stays bound because they believe forgiveness must be earned, but mercy cannot be purchased, it is received. When you embrace mercy, condemnation loses its hold. You stop rehearsing old failures and begin rehearsing truth. Each morning becomes proof that God's compassion renews daily. Embracing mercy means releasing self-criticism and accepting restoration. It realigns your worth with God's word, not your wounds. Let mercy silence accusations and rewrite your internal dialogue with love. Every time you fail forward, grace is already waiting to lift you.

F – Fast, Pray & Surrender

Fasting purifies motives and reorders desires. It dismantles distractions and forces dependence. When you fast, you declare that your appetite bows to your assignment. Prayer becomes sharper because hunger clarifies hearing. Surrender aligns timelines, you stop begging for speed and start trusting God's sequence. In fasting, control dies so peace can rise. Replace striving with stillness; let silence preach louder than requests. Each act of surrender becomes a seed of obedience, watered by prayer, and matured by faith. True surrender does not seek outcomes; it seeks alignment. When you rest, He refines. When you yield, He leads.

I – Identify Soul Ties

Every attachment carries influence. Some ties feed your spirit; others drain it. Identifying soul ties means asking God to expose emotional, relational, or mental bonds that hinder progress. Old conversations, shared pain, or digital connections can still occupy spiritual space. You can't be full of God and still tied to Egypt. Detachment is not rejection, it is deliverance. Allow God to cut cords to counterfeit intimacy so real connection can flow. Release every memory that still governs emotion. What once felt familiar may now be a chain. Identification precedes freedom; clarity precedes cleansing. Your wholeness demands separation.

N – Nurture Your Identity

Identity must be fed to stay firm. Speak life until truth becomes instinct. Nurturing your identity means choosing words that align with heaven, not history. Read the Word until it becomes your mirror. Refuse labels that contradict God's definition of you. Growth happens when you feed faith more than fear. Surround yourself with environments that affirm destiny, not doubt. When you nurture identity, insecurity loses its influence. You live rooted, not reactive; focused, not fractured. Identity is not maintained by emotion but by meditation, on scripture, on promise, on purpose. Daily nurturing produces unshakable confidence in Christ.

E – Establish Godly Boundaries

Boundaries protect what blessing built. They guard peace, purity, and power. Establishing boundaries means saying yes to purpose and no to distraction. Boundaries are gates, not walls, they discern what enters your garden. Godly boundaries keep you available to Him without being accessible to everything else. Protect your time, your thoughts, and your temple. Holiness requires structure. When boundaries are weak, temptation thrives. Strengthen your "no" so your "yes" retains authority. The boundary around your calling determines the longevity of your anointing. Protect what costs you to carry. Peace is proof that your walls are working.

D – Develop a Covenant Lifestyle

Covenant living is consistency wrapped in consecration. It means daily obedience in health, finances, and worship. A covenant life refuses compromise. It treats every decision as a reflection of devotion. Development happens through small, steady obedience, choosing prayer over panic, tithing over impulse, purity over popularity. Covenant means God can trust your yes tomorrow as much as today. When lifestyle aligns with lordship, favor follows function. The covenant life is not glamorous; it is grounded. It builds legacy through discipline and devotion. Live in rhythm with heaven's standards. Covenant is where calling matures into character.

Your story may differ, but your refining requires the same ingredients: fire, faith, and follow-through.

The Hardest Step: "F – Fast, Pray & Surrender"

Fasting tested me in ways comfort never could. It stripped away every illusion of control and revealed what still ruled my heart. When I began fasting consistently, I was in pain physically from IIH, emotionally from betrayal, and financially from barely surviving. Yet, in those weakened places, God required more of me. I was sowing seeds while bills stacked high, giving while my cupboards felt empty, praying through pain that blurred my vision.

At first, I thought fasting would earn me favor. I treated it like a transaction; if I gave up enough, maybe God would bless me faster. But fasting exposed me instead. It revealed hidden idols I had dressed in good intentions. My emotional spending masked loneliness. My constant giving masked my fear of lack. My prayers were often driven by panic, not purity. Fasting confronted all of it.

Surrender wasn't poetic, it was painful. There were nights I sat in my prayer chair trembling from hunger, tears mixing with prayer. My flesh wanted comfort, but my spirit craved cleansing. I realized fasting was not about withholding food; it was about weakening flesh so spirit could lead. Each skipped meal became a mirror, showing where I still depended on things instead of God.

The daily wrestle between flesh and spirit was fierce. My body ached, my emotions swung, but something holy was happening. The more I emptied myself, the more He filled me. When I fasted, clarity replaced confusion. When I prayed, peace replaced panic. When I surrendered timelines, He reordered my steps.

God's voice grew louder in the silence of sacrifice. He showed me how emotional appetites, food, scrolling, conversations, had dulled my sensitivity to His whisper. Every time I laid something down, He revealed what I had picked up in its place. I learned that fasting is warfare in disguise. It dethrones self and enthrones Spirit.

Through fasting, God broke agreements I had made with fear. He exposed how I used productivity to prove worth. He redefined provision, not as abundance of things, but alignment with His will. When I released control, I found communion. When I released striving, I found strength.

Fasting didn't make life easier; it made faith real. It taught me that discipline sustains what desire begins. It trained my spirit to submit when my flesh wanted to quit.

The crushing became communion. The hunger became holiness. The fasting became fire.

The Easiest Step: "I – Identity"

For years, I lived defined by what I did instead of who I was. Teacher. Mother. Leader. Giver. Every title carried responsibility, but none carried rest. I performed well in every role yet felt unseen at my core. My value rose and fell with how productive or needed I felt. I thought calling meant constant motion until the Holy Spirit whispered one morning, *"You are not just My servant—you are My daughter."*

That revelation dismantled everything I built on self-worth. When I rediscovered who I am in Christ, striving stopped. I didn't need to earn belonging; I already had it. I learned that identity is not achieved, it is received. My name in heaven carried more weight than any platform on earth. The peace that followed this realization anchored me deeper than applause ever could.

Knowing I am a daughter steadied me when visibility increased. It kept my heart pure when attention grew louder. Identity tamed ambition by reminding me that success without surrender is still failure in disguise. When I wanted to chase opportunities, God would say, *"Stay seated in sonship."* That posture protected me from performance. I stopped chasing validation and started walking in revelation.

When ministry expanded and prophetic doors opened, I no longer introduced myself by function. I carried presence instead of pressure. Identity rooted my prophetic walk, it reminded me that power flows from proximity, not publicity. Titles shift with seasons, but daughterhood never expires.

During the season described in *The Prophetess Awakens*, identity became the foundation of my mantle. I understood that God was not crowning me for visibility but commissioning me for intimacy. My authority began where my adoption was secured.

I no longer pray to prove. I pray because I belong. Everything changed the day I stopped working for approval and started walking from acceptance.

Living a Covenant Lifestyle

Covenant living means being set apart, not perfect. It is a lifestyle of daily consecration, ordinary obedience done with extraordinary consistency. It's not about flawless performance but faithful posture. A covenant life reflects loyalty to God when no one is watching and reverence for His presence in every decision. The goal is not control; it is communion.

A covenant lifestyle isn't a checklist; it's a daily bowing of the heart. Every rhythm of your day becomes worship when done with intention. These small disciplines create an environment where faith matures and holiness becomes practical, not abstract.

Morning Sh'ma: Listen before speaking.

Each day begins with stillness. Before messages, before movement, whisper, *"Speak, Lord, your servant is listening."* This first act of attention tunes your spirit before you face distraction. It reminds you that hearing from Heaven outranks hustling for approval.

Weekly Fasting & Worship: Replace appetite with adoration.

Dedicate time weekly to abstain, from food, social media, or noise, and fill that space with worship. Fasting becomes fire when it's fueled by devotion, not deprivation. It resets your appetite for God's presence above every craving for comfort.

Financial Stewardship: Intentional sowing, not impulsive spending.

Covenant stewardship manages resources with prayer, not pressure. Every seed sown; every dollar spent should carry purpose. Emotional giving leads to regret; intentional giving leads to harvest. Stewardship honors God's order and builds discipline that outlasts emotion.

Scriptural Confession: "I am refined, not ruined."

Words create worlds. Speak what aligns with your identity, not your insecurity. Confession is agreement with Heaven. When life feels unstable, declaration restores direction. What you say over yourself sets the tone for your atmosphere.

Prophetic Journaling: Tracking divine dialogue.

Record what God reveals, dreams, impressions, answered prayers. Writing becomes witness. Journaling anchors revelation that could otherwise drift away in distraction. Over time, you'll see a pattern of God's faithfulness written in your own hand.

Sabbath Rest: Rest equals warfare.

Resting is not retreating, it's resisting burnout. Sabbath is sacred resistance to culture's demand for constant output. When you rest, Heaven works on your behalf. Rest is a weapon that restores strength and sharpens discernment.

Community & Accountability: Refinement happens in fellowship, not isolation.

Isolation distorts, but community refines. Stay connected to people who challenge you to stay pure, grounded, and teachable. Accountability isn't control, it's protection. Iron sharpens iron only through contact.

Commit your way to the Lord, work wholeheartedly, and stay faithful in fellowship. Covenant living turns consistency into consecration.

Devotional Insights

Prophetic Declarations

- I am refined, not ruined.

- The fire didn't destroy me; it developed me.

- I release control and rest in divine timing.

- My hunger births holiness.

- I am a daughter of covenant, sealed by grace.

- My story is oil that heals others.

- Every test became a testimony.

- Every delay produced discipline.

- The crushing was not for my defeat but for my consecration.

- I am trusted with trials because I am chosen for transformation.

- My obedience carries fragrance.

- My faith still moves mountains.

- My altar remains burning.

- I am steadfast, surrendered, and sealed for glory.

- I live refined, whole, holy, and ready.

Journal Prompts

1. What's one area God is asking you to **fast from**, not just **pray for**?

2. Which letter of **REFINED** do you sense God revisiting in your life right now?

3. Write a **covenant statement** for the next thirty days: "Lord, I will ————— as a sign of surrender."

REFINED is not a checklist; it is a rhythm of relationship. Every stage, reflection, surrender, discipline, identity, is a continual cycle of grace. Refinement repeats because holiness matures through repetition. You never graduate from formation; you grow deeper into it. The process is not about perfection but about proximity. When you live refined, you live ready.

The fire shaped your faith. The pruning guarded your purity. The fasting taught you to focus. Every refining moment built a foundation for glory. What once felt like breaking has become building.

So, rise, daughter of fire. You've been crushed, but not consumed. You've been purified, but not disqualified. You are His reflection, radiant, refined, and ready to rebuild. The same God who refined you will now release you.

Thank you for walking this wilderness with me, for letting your tears become oil and your obedience become offering. The world does not need another influencer. It needs refined intercessors, women who carry fire without compromise and oil without mixture. Keep your altar burning. Keep your heart bowed low. You are not striving anymore; you are sealed for glory.

Closing Prayer

Lord, thank You for the fire that formed me. Where my flesh resists, strengthen my spirit. Burn away idols, refine my motives, and teach me to fast with purpose, not performance. Let my hunger be holy, my surrender sincere, and my obedience immediate. Seal my heart in covenant with You. May every yes carry Heaven's fragrance, every word carry Your fire, and every day mirror Your glory. Anchor my thoughts in purity and my hands in purpose. I yield all timelines, titles, and fears at Your feet. Refine me again until only You remain. Let the oil you pressed from my pain heal others. Keep my altar burning and my spirit bowed low before You. In Jesus' name, **Amen.**

Conclusion

We walked through the wilderness and found oil in the fire. Every chapter carried its own altar, breaking, pruning, pressing, becoming, and finally, commissioning. You didn't just read these pages; you endured them with me. Together we've touched the ache of surrender and discovered that what once wounded us has now anointed us. Each tear became seed, each scar became sermon. The wilderness taught obedience, the pressing revealed purity, and the crushing unlocked covenant. Now we stand together at the altar, not who we were, but who we've become: refined, radiant, and ready to pour again.

The wilderness was never punishment; it was preparation. Every pruning stripped what pride built. Every pressing produced purity. Every crushing proved you were chosen. Refinement revealed that pain was not God's absence but His attention. What you lost in the wilderness became oil for nations. What broke you became what blessed you. The fire that tested you also trusted you with glory. Refinement was never about survival; it was about stewardship. You were not just being rescued; you were being refined for responsibility. Heaven used every hardship as holy training for what you now carry with grace.

Today, I live surrendered, still learning, still set apart. I am no longer the girl who survived; I am the woman who was sealed. Refinement continues daily as God polishes what He already purified. My yes remains tender, my altar still burning, and my oil still costly. The same fire that once broke me now burns through me with purpose. Every day, I relearn dependence, rediscover peace, and remain at His feet. I write these final words not as someone who has arrived but as someone still becoming, and I'll meet you somewhere in the process of obedience.

Now it's your turn to rise. Your wilderness has an assignment. Every scar carries instruction, and every delay hides divine design. Build your altar. Protect your oil. Live refined. The REFINED framework is not a rulebook; it's a rhythm of relationship that keeps your heart close to God. You are not behind; you are in process. Keep walking, even when the fire feels familiar. What you carry costs Heaven something, so steward it with reverence. Walk boldly into your next season as one who knows her oil cost something. Let your obedience speak louder than your fear, and your purity shine brighter than your pain. The refining never ends, it only deepens your anointing.

Purity remains the heartbeat of this book. Purity isn't just abstaining, it's abiding. The oil only flows where the heart stays pure. Live in daily communion through worship, fasting, and obedience. Keep your altar burning and your motives clean. Stay at the altar long enough for God to speak again. Presence is the new platform; intimacy is influence. Those who linger with Him carry what crowds can't manufacture, authentic oil that smells like surrender, not performance.

Final Benediction: A Prophetic Blessing

May the oil that was pressed from your pain never run dry.

May your voice carry healing, your hands carry fire, and your heart remain pure.

May you lead with wisdom, love with holiness, and serve with joy.

May your wilderness turn into worship, your crushing into communion, and your story into glory.

You are refined, not ruined, and anointed for such a time as this.

I am refined, restored, and released.

I will carry the oil with honor.

I am sealed for glory, and I will pour again.

This is not goodbye; it's the beginning of your next "yes."

The oil still flows; from my altar to yours.

— Josette, Blossom Refined

ABOUT THE AUTHOR

Josette Fleury (*Blossom Refined*) is a Haitian American mother, educator, intercessor, and prophetic voice whose life has been refined by fire and restored by grace. Known online as Blossom Refined, she encourages women through transparent storytelling and Bible-centered teaching on identity, healing, and holiness.

Her debut, *The Refining Room: Devotional Memoir: 90-Day Journey for Women Breaking, Becoming & Being Set Apart*, invites readers to move from pain to purpose through a practical framework for spiritual renewal. With over two decades in education as a teacher, mentor, and assistant principal, Josette brings biblical wisdom and relatable compassion to her ministry.

She writes for women who feel disqualified or overlooked and for anyone ready to trade shame for freedom, confusion for clarity, and survival for true transformation.

When not writing or interceding for others, Josette lives a lifestyle of worship, fasting, and prayer both globally and from her home in Queens, New York. Connect with her on TikTok and YouTube at *@BlossomRefined* for weekly encouragement, prayers, and teachings.

Contact Page

Author: Josette Fleury (Blossom Refined)

Website: https://josettefleury.com

Social Media:

TikTok: @blossomrefined

YouTube: @blossomrefined

Facebook: facebook.com/therefiningroombook

Instagram: @inclusivelyinspired

Pinterest: The Refining Room

For Booking, Collaborations, Or Speaking Engagements:

Visit: https://josettefleury.com

BEFORE YOU GO...
Can I Ask a Small Favor?

If you enjoyed this book, your review means the world to me.
Click the link or scan the QR code below:

Leave a Review:

https://www.amazon.com/review/create-review?asin=B0G3X6DWH5

www.ingramcontent.com/pod-product-compliance
Lightning Source LLC
Chambersburg PA
CBHW051516120626
46551CB00012B/956